BEAR ATTACKS OF THE CENTURY

BEAR ATTACKS OF THE CENTURY

True Stories of Courage and Survival

Larry Mueller and Marguerite Reiss

The Lyons Press
Guilford, Connecticut

An imprint of The Globe Pequot Press

The Lyons Press is an imprint of The Globe Pequot Press.

A majority of the pieces here appeared in slightly different form in *Outdoor Life* magazine.

Printed in the United States of America
10 9 8 7 6 5 4 3 2

Designed by Sheryl Kober

Library of Congress Cataloging-in Publication Data

Mueller, Larry.
Bear attacks of the century : true stories of courage and survival /
Larry Mueller and Marguerite Reiss.
p. cm.
ISBN 1-59228-270-9 (trade pbk.)
1. Bear attacks—Anecdotes. I. Reiss, Marguerite. II. Title.

QL737.C27M84 2005
599.78'156'6—dc22

2005040749

Larry:

To Micky, my perfect wife of fifty-five years, who has suffered a bear of an attack from the most dreaded malady in our society. And to the Cedar Ridge saints, the kind, loving, and so incredibly patient nurses and nurses aids at Cedar Ridge Healthcare Center who are caring for her around the clock since it became abundantly clear that, despite our determination to do so, my daughter, Anne, and I could not accomplish it ourselves.

Marguerite:

To William Wennen, M.D. FACS. The stories here are pain-filled almost beyond human endurance. But to Alaska surgeon Bill Wennen, the iron thread that runs through bear attacks is courage by contagion—a quality akin to empathy, which brings hundreds to his office offering whatever they can to help victims of bear maulings.

To Drs. Glenn and Eva Oids. Constantly on the lookout to make others' lives better. To them I am inexpressibly grateful for the chance to write and sell adventure stories on the Last Frontier.

To Frances Halpern, host of *Beyond Words* on KCLU, an NPR affiliate, moderator for the *Los Angeles Times* Festival of Books, former *Los Angeles Times* columnist; a relentless cheerleader of my writing.

And to Bruce Barbour of Barbour Books, a colleague who believed.

CONTENTS

ACKNOWLEDGMENTS

To editors Richard Schneider, Vin Sparano, Fulton Oursler Jr., Ken Gilmore, Mary Aikins, Marlane Liddell, Laurie Harper of the Sebastian Agency; and Alaska outdoors writer, Craig Medfred. To encouragers Melinda Milheim, B. J. Krevitz, Col. Eric Wheaton, Lowell Thomas Jr., Larry Hausmann, Dr. Ted and Ellie Rubin, Eunice Borrelli. To writers Jan Ingram, Dalene Perrigo, Thetus Smith, Doris Thomas, Dianne Barske, Susan Ohrberg, Asta Corley, Carol Sturgulewski, Millie Spezialy, Carolyn Rinehart, Elaine Williamson, Emily McKenzie, Pat Richardson, Ella Wright.To doctors Charles Herndon, Donna Chester, Fred Hillman, Mark Mills, James Schafer, Arthur Manoli, Jeff Morin. To members of the New York City Explorers Club, the Alaska Press Women, the Red Cedar Friends Meeting and Unitarian Church, both of Lansing, Michigan, and to Calvin Kern for constant, generous help.

INTRODUCTION

Bear Attacks of the Century is a book that opens a fearful wound as old as man himself. We can indeed imagine how it felt to be slower, weaker, and too lacking in jaw to bite back in a world populated with huge, efficient predators. And it's unpleasant to be reminded that even today there's a chance that something may want to eat us any time we enter bear country. Nobody reads a bear attack story and says, "Wow! What an adventure! I'd like to try that." Yet, by something deep within, we seem drawn to the primeval nature of bear attacks. I call it a community survival instinct, developed by eons of dodging large animal jaws. We are encouraged when we hear that a victim fought courageously and won. Or we express admiration when the victim's partner coolly maneuvers in position and waits for a shot that will kill the bear, but not his buddy. And it's heartwarming to know that there are others out there, friends and strangers alike, who unhesitatingly take heroic measures to evacuate the victim, get him to an appropriate hospital, or just show up and wait in line to give him lifesaving blood.

Nevertheless, as might be expected, not everyone has inherited the community survival instinct. So far, however, we've only found one example. Bruce Brown, an archer since high school, thought that the ultimate hunting challenge would be taking a grizzly by bow and arrow. His coworker and hunting buddy, David Delapina, would accompany him as backup. According to 1990 newspaper accounts, both carried short-barreled 12-gauge pump shotguns loaded with three-inch slugs. Bruce also carried a shoulder-holstered .44 Magnum semiautomatic pistol under his left arm.

The two split up to double their chances of spotting a bear. Seeing a young grizzly walk out onto a gravel bar, Bruce approached to about twenty yards, and accurately placed an arrow into its vitals. The bear made it into thick brush before dropping dead. Bruce went back for David, and the men returned to find two more bears on the scene. David suggested they back off. Bruce didn't follow his suggestion. David did back off about twenty yards. One of the bears, looking straight at Bruce, started walking toward him. At thirty yards, Bruce fired a warning shot, which prompted the bear to charge. Taking one step backward, Bruce's feet tangled in brush and he fell, jamming dirt into his shotgun's receiver. It didn't matter. In a thirty-yard run, a bear can be on top of a man before he can pump another shell into the chamber.

The bear grabbed Bruce by the head and swung him in a half circle, and then let go, apparently because it didn't like the feel of the right hand that Bruce managed to shove into its mouth. It crunched the hand. Bruce kicked the bear and got swung by the leg. With Bruce yelling for help, David fired a shot and missed. He pumped the shotgun and pulled the trigger again, but nothing happened. The bear turned its head and looked at David, who thought he was next. Believing that his gun had jammed (more likely he had short stroked the pump action, and the second shell had not reached the chamber) he ran—and didn't stop until he had climbed into a tree stand that he had seen earlier.

Finally, a badly battered Bruce managed to twist his left hand enough to pull the pistol from the holster under his left arm. Firing several shots, he broke the bear's neck. Bruce called for David who had heard the shots, but didn't hear the calling and thought Bruce was dead. David stayed up the tree while Bruce struggled back to the truck and drove it thirty miles to a ranger station. Bruce understood why David might run away from the bear to safely unjam his gun, but he couldn't understand why David didn't return to help. Michael Carey of the Anchorage *Daily News* best summed up how most people who know bears feel about what David did: "It's perfectly understandable and equally unforgivable."

One other point I'd like to make is that readers sometimes expect outdoor ordeal stories to be sensationalized. Not in this book. Bear attacks are horrible enough just as they happen. In fact, we have taken great pains to avoid phrases that could be labeled hyperbole. We have also given great attention to detail. Marguerite lived in Alaska and still visits annually. She finds most of the stories and runs them past me. If we both agree that all elements of an outstanding story are there, she begins taping interviews, and then sends me a word-for-word transcript. Although I have the story in the victim's exact words, few people tell their tales in chronological order. They may start in the middle of the attack, then switch back and forth with bits and pieces of how it came about and how it ended. It's my job to reassemble the parts in logical sequence. We often find pieces missing, so Marguerite does a bit more interviewing. By now, we essentially have the story, but some details may not quite ring true to me, possibly because I'm a lifelong outdoorsman and Marguerite, an excellent writer and interviewer, would rather see large animals through bars of cages. So it's my turn to talk with the people involved and get fine details that make me think I can clearly see it happening. After it's written, they get a copy to read for accuracy. Only when they are satisfied that it reads exactly as it occurred does it go to the editor. We have exaggerated nothing. Nor have we glossed over anything. Horrifying as the encounters were, what you read is what these people experienced.

Larry Mueller
December 2004

Adrenaline flows differently in bear attacks. People do almost superhuman things to survive. But equally amazing are the heroics of those around the victims. It is as if evolution has provided us with . . .

COURAGE BY CONTAGION

Do bear attacks touch people in the far-back recesses of their psyches? Reach latent ancestral memories of cave days when humans were potential prey?

Indeed, there are those who say that their nightmares involved bears before they ever saw one—either alive or on film. Among youngsters exposed to long hours of television from early on, such uninfluenced dreams become difficult to verify. But an older man recalls a recurring childhood dream in Technicolor: him in slow motion, being chased by a bear up a spiraling mountain road—long before he had seen either bear *or* mountain.

"Whatever it is," says Dr. William Wennen, the Fairbanks trauma/plastic surgeon who reconstructs a majority of Alaska's bear attack victims, "I can tell you that something very different happens when there's a bear attack. We might have a bus wreck with twenty people injured and needing blood. We put out the call and always get enough blood.

"But let just one person be attacked by a bear, and people flood the waiting room. My wife, Emily, works in the blood bank at the hospital, so we're very aware of this. In one case, the call went out via radio in late afternoon. Within an hour there were nearly fifty *more* volunteers than we needed. They didn't worry about dinner. Children were along because parents hadn't taken time to find a sitter. And they stayed until we could positively assure them that the victim was stabilized and their blood wouldn't be required."

The tremendous courage of victims is another phenomenon. "People injured in auto wrecks tend to crawl off and wait for help," says Dr. Wennen. "But adrenalin flows differently in bear attacks. People do almost superhuman things to survive."

Ralph Borders (see "The Grizzly Jinx") had both arms chewed, two-thirds of his upper lip missing to his nose, both legs bitten, and claw damage to his body. Yet he pulled his hat down to hold together the torn flesh on his head, and walked five miles back to spike camp where, luckily, the packer was still around and could horseback him two more miles to the cabins of other sheep hunters.

"In bear attacks, the human survival instinct is extraordinary," says the doctor who sees the terrible punishment they live through.

Jim Mariotte (See "Ceaseless Terror") was attacked and mauled by a grizzly while caping out a moose head. When playing dead didn't work, he slammed his skinning knife into the attacker's neck. The surprised bear backed off only to charge again, cut his tongue trying to bite at the knife, and once more got the knife sunk into the same place. By the third charge, Marriotte was on his feet, despite chewed buttocks and damag s. This time, the bear left with the knife still sticking in his neck.

In another display of raw courage, Donald Coverston fought back with the only weapon he had—a hand ax. According to newspaper accounts, he slammed the charging grizzly between the eyes, and then lost the ax. The bear attacked two more times until Coverston finally played dead. For him, this tactic worked.

"Patricia Whiting-O'Keefe," said Dr. Wennen, "suffered the worst attack and displayed the greatest courage of any of the victims I've reconstructed. One eye was out on her cheek. Facial bones were smashed. Her nose was gone. Half of her scalp was missing. She had lost well over half of her blood. Massive swipes had ripped her legs and buttocks. And the bear had broken through the skull, actually exposing a part of her brain. She had survived all this for twenty-four hours before she got here. Yet this small woman was not only coherent, she was poised and very much a lady—a very remarkable lady."

Patricia, a Ph.D. in computer science, her husband Quinn O'Keefe, M.D., and his high school friend Chad Hansen, a professor of Chinese philosophy, had been flown to the north slope of the Brooks Range for two weeks of backpacking, camping, and wildlife photography. They had camped at the Lake Peters Research Station until Dr. Fisher and his wife flew in to do some research for the U.S. Fish and Wildlife Service. Rather than camp on someone's doorstep, they moved their campsite to the junction of lakes Schrader and Peters. Finally, they decided on a three-day excursion to the Hulahula River, which flows from the Brooks Range into the Beaufort Sea.

Backpacking across the rolling tundra proved arduous. Progress was slow. Muck-bottomed tundra bowls pockmarked the landscape. Mud sucked back at boots with every step that couldn't be made on somewhat higher tussocks. Finally, at nightfall, the three reached Katak Lake, which drains into the Hulahula, and set up camp.

Next morning they headed cross country with day packs, now about twenty miles from the research station. At one point, Quinn and Chad stopped to photograph Arctic ground squirrels. Pat continued on about a hundred yards over a rise and out of sight. Suddenly, a noise. She turned to see a grizzly sow with three cubs in full charge at fifteen yards.

With amazing clarity, Pat remembers all that happened in the next few seconds. Bears can charge at thirty-five miles an hour. If this grizzly were only going thirty, it covered those fifteen yards in one second. But the mind of a threatened human is even faster. Whiting-O'Keefe says her thoughts in that one second were: "It's a female thinking she has to protect her cubs. Humans can't outrun bears. Running invites chase. Sometimes bears bluff with fake charges. She's too close to expect that. When grizzlies perceive they've eliminated the threat, they often halt the attack and leave."

Incredibly, she even had time to notice the beauty of the animal. Its hair was thick and shimmering, appearing auburn at first, but then multicolored, dark brown with reddish tips, as it neared. Her cubs were miniatures of her, except their eyes were wide with wonder. Hers reflected only single-purpose determination.

With one *woof*, the bear signaled her cubs to run on, and in a rare move for an attacking grizzly, she stopped, stood up, and bent down to attack. Pat tried to cover her head with her arms. "I saw her eyes focused on me and her mouth agape as her jaws closed over my head and face," she said. "I pushed up at her. I heard bone crunch. I perceived my flesh being torn away, but I didn't actually feel it at the time."

She collapsed to the ground, arms over her head, in a calculated attempt to appear dead. She tried not to breathe. As bears do, the sow swiped the sensitive genital area to test for signs of life. With incredible control, Pat took the slashes across the buttocks and legs without moving. After an eternity packed into a few minutes, she moved slightly to test the situation. The bear was gone.

"Few bear attack victims are as cool and controlled as Pat," Dr. Wennen said, "but equally amazing are the heroics and seemingly superhuman efforts of those around the victims. It's as if evolution has provided us with courage by contagion."

Hearing Pat scream, Quinn and Chad ran over the rise towards her, only to be confronted and chased back by another sow with two cubs. Agonizingly, they hid until she left, certain that Pat would die unless they got to her in one piece.

Quinn assessed her condition and stayed to care for her as best he could with what he had. Chad ran back to camp, traded boots for tennis shoes, raced across the tundra that had been so difficult to walk, and by some miracle of spirit covered those twenty miles back to Lake Peters Research Station in five hours.

Despite the fog rolling in and the possibility that he couldn't land again if it thickened, Dr. Fisher took off in his plane. The men agreed that Chad should stay below. The rescue helicopter might need him to locate the O'Keefes. Fisher spiraled up to the necessary altitude and radioed Deadhorse.

Pilot Matt Kato received the message. He knew that Walt Audi had circled the area in a Cessna 185 and reported fog extending into the Brooks Range, which would cover the O'Keefes' location. Nevertheless, Kato and ARCO's Dr. William Worrell concluded that they had to try.

Kato assumed a heading for Schrader Lake using the Deadhorse VOR reception. From there, navigation through the fog was by dead reckoning—using time, distance, and heading to get them to Katak Lake. Flying at about a hundred feet, they were lucky enough to find the campsite in the fog. But where were the O'Keefes? To avoid wasting precious time and fuel, Kato flew to the research station to pick up Chad. Starting again at the campsite, Chad pointed the way.

By then it was 10:00 or 11:00 P.M. In the low light of a setting sun, they could barely make their way through the fog. Suddenly, they spotted an orange glow off to the right. Quinn had heard the helicopter and, making best use of what he had at hand, signaled by setting fire to a wad of toilet paper in his hat.

With the fuel gauge at "bingo" (just enough for the return trip) Pat was evacuated. Quinn and Chad returned to the research station, this time taking eight hours instead of five. Walt Audi buzzed the station in his wheeled-plane to alert the men to his partner, Gil Zimansky, who was landing with a floatplane. "Hurry," Zimansky said. "Get in before the hole closes in the fog."

It closed. But Zimansky said, "Don't worry. I know where the mountain is. I'll bank to the left before I hit it." And so he did.

"No pilot in his right mind would fly in that kind of soup," said Dr. Wennen. "This *is* truly courage by contagion. When it's a bear attack, people bend every rule in the book."

And so it also was with the helicopter pilot who evacuated Ralph Borders. With needle on empty, he flew through a snow squall because there weren't enough fumes left to lift over or fly around it. And Leroy Sewell somehow ran four and a half miles through snow as deep as his knees to summon the helicopter by radio-telephone.

According to Dr. Wennen, only one hunter in the last twenty years, despite being armed, panicked and left his partner with the bear.

Quite the opposite, two embarrassed sheep hunters (who shall remain nameless) foolishly decided to sleep on a well-used bear trail in sleeping bags in order to be on-site for the next morning's hunt. One awoke to being mauled by a grizzly. He tried to roll away and, by luck, tumbled down the steep slope, rifle still inside his bag. The bear turned to attack his buddy. The hunter downslope struggled free of the bag, but then could not get a clear shot without the risk of hitting his partner. In desperation, he began yelling to draw the bear's attention to himself. His courage worked. He shot the bear as it charged downhill.

"When I moved to Alaska in 1975," said Dr. Wennen, "I wanted to teach my son, Eric, then eight, to hunt. But hunting the Alaskan wilderness is vastly different from what I had been taught. One stupid little mistake puts you right on the ragged edge of survival. I didn't want to do something stupid. So I took a University of Alaska course given by a guide, Joe Want. He taught us to err on the side of caution. Operating room experience taught me the terrible reality of what *can* happen. I began to build in redundancy—caution upon caution—not to worry hunting into becoming a horrible experience, but to maintain preparedness so it *doesn't* become a horrible experience."

Over the years, Bill Wennen has evolved a sort of "Stupid Is" list, starting with the standard, "Stupid is not wearing your seatbelt." His list continues:

Stupid is not learning bear behavior.

Stupid is not carrying a lightweight assembly of first-aid materials to treat most eventualities.

Stupid is hunting in bear country with calibers that are too small. (Dr. Wennen now hunts with a .460 Weatherby, which has accounted for twelve moose and a walrus—back when they were legal—all one-shot kills. Many hunters carry a .357 Magnum or .44 Magnum as backup sidearms. Either has considerably less muzzle energy than the little .30/30. Wennen, on Joe Want's advice, carries the largest caliber handgun he can shoot without becoming afraid of it—a .475 Linebaugh.

Stupid is hunting solo. (Joe said buddy-hunt, and stay together. Decide each day who will take the first shot. In case of attack, or when hunting grizzlies, both hunters keep shooting until no possibility exists that the bear will get up looking for who hurt it.)

Stupid is the advice that unarmed hikers should wear little tinkle bells on their backpacks. (Patricia O'Keefe wore these "bear bells." Rattling rocks in cans may be more effective in warning bears to slip away before a confrontation. The supervisor of a salmon tagging program found police whistles useless, so then went to small gas-powered boat horns. No more bears were seen until some crews stopped tooting. They promptly ran into streamside bears again.)

Stupid is camping unarmed—especially in nothing more than sleeping bags in parks where hunting prohibitions have caused bears to lose their fear of humans. (Park areas demanding this—and desk-bound supervisors forcing surveyors to work unarmed in grizzly territory—is attempted homicide in Dr. Wennen's book.)

Stupid is hiking unarmed, either solo or in pairs. (There are no known grizzly attacks on groups of three or more, provided all members stayed together.)

Interestingly, the courageous spirit that Dr. Wennen sees does not end with the attack. Rarely has a mauling stopped anyone from hunting again at the first opportunity. And rarely has a hunter wanted revenge. Almost invariably, they say it wasn't the bear's fault. They were hunting in the bear's territory, and it only did what nature programmed bears to do. In fact, vicious as the attacks have seemed, when compared to what grizzlies regularly do to natural prey and to each other (knock heads off thick-necked animals with single swipes of the paws or inflict lethal damage to the powerful structures of their own kind), human mauling seems strangely inhibited.

Must-Know Bear Behavior

Nobody wants to either provoke an attack or kill bears unnecessarily. To avoid either, be aware that most maulings occur when humans unwittingly get too close to a bear guarding its kill or to a sow protecting her cubs. These situations are difficult to predict, and produce a greater number of attacks and fewer false charges than do chance encounters. Surprise encounters might be defused by not making eye contact (considered a challenge), by not running (which invites chase), and, if you're armed, by firing into the ground to halt a charge. Be cautious about yelling at bears. If it doesn't intimidate them into retreating, yelling will likely provoke an attack.

When a bear attacks in earnest, it goes for the head—unless the person is running. In that case, it grabs the buttocks and shakes its victim like dogs shake rabbits—which is severely damaging to connective tissue. In case after case, the bear has then backed off to wait, watch, and again resume attack to the body and sometimes head, especially when it sees slight movement. Most bears will wait and watch once more, then swipe their claws across the genital area to test for signs of life. Most grizzlies leave the victim when they're convinced that they've eliminated the threat.

This attack behavior justifies the often heard advice to "play dead." It is the unarmed person's *only* defense. Unfortunately, although rarely, the attack can be lethal before it ends. Even rarer is the grizzly that considers humans as food. But it did happen to Jay B. L. Reeves in 1974, Alan Precup in 1976, John Tesinsky in 1986, and Harley Sievenpiper in 1988. A properly armed marksman is not likely to risk the possible results of playing dead.

After an Attack

"When bears bite, it's not like you bite off a piece of cookie," says Dr. Bill Wennen. "They shake, twist, rip, and pull. Tremendous damage is done deeply in the tissues. But the puncture wounds are bad enough. And the average person wants to wash them out, pull them together, and bind or tape them shut. *Don't!* Bears' teeth and claws are full of exotic bacteria. Clean the wounds, and keep them clean until help arrives. But you'll never get them clean enough to close. Let that be for the surgeon, or you'll cause serious infection."

Don't load up victims with heavy food. Bacon and eggs will sit in the stomach for days until blood pressure, circulation, and other vital body functions are back to normal. Regurgitating worries anesthesiologists. You may allow victims to suck on hard candy or Lifesavers, but make sure they don't fall asleep and choke. Give no food at all if they'll reach the hospital within six hours. Purified or boiled water is okay, but warm it to help avoid hypothermia. No alcohol. No milk because of the fat. No aspirin—it promotes bleeding. Tylenol is okay for pain. No iodine in the wounds. Ordinary soap is okay. Clorox is too harsh. Hydrogen peroxide is somewhat harsh and should not be used in deep wounds when expectations for early rescue are high. When a doctor sees gas in the wound, he immediately thinks of gas gangrene, a surgical emergency sometimes necessitating amputation.

Keep the victim covered and warm. No tourniquets. A wounded limb can be raised to minimize bleeding without closing the punctures and tears. But raise the feet only if necessary. And don't raise a wounded head to slow bleeding. Sooner or later the victim will pass out from shock.

Stay with the victim and provide calm, cheerful moral support.

Wilderness Survival Kit

Bandannas bought or made in fluorescent orange are high on Dr. Wennen's list. They can be used for rescue signals, slings, ties for stick splints, and binding to hold a loose scalp. They can be tied at the corners to carry things. They can be used for warmth, or to slow bleeding.

Sanitary water is essential. The danger of *Giardia*, animal-borne parasitic intestinal protozoa, is everywhere. *Giardia* causes intense stomach pain, and causes food to pass through the body in minutes. Many purification tablets don't touch it. Water can be boiled. Dr. Wennen also carries a Katadyn filter to camp. "If the water is muddy, if you scoop up a bucket of water, let the silt settle before filtering to avoid clogging the device," he advises.

Dr. Wennen carries one Ace bandage, a fairly broad-spectrum antibiotic, salt, Bacitracin ointment, Tylenol, and soap. He advises against requesting from doctors, or using, the stronger narcotic-type painkillers. They have serious side effects, including impaired judgment, depressed respiration, and lawsuits against well-meaning helpers when something goes wrong.

"Keep in mind that everything weighs something," Dr. Wennen concludes. "Keep it simple to be able to carry the essentials."

CEASELESS TERROR

Jim Mariotte tried to play it by the book. Don't move. Act dead. But the grizzly ignored the rules, attacked again, and hooked a canine tooth over his kneecap and into the joint. Playing possum wasn't Jim's style, anyhow. He angrily jerked upward, cursing loudly and stabbing his three-and-three-quarter-inch skinning knife repeatedly into the neck of the bear that was almost in his face.

Jim Mariotte, forty-one, sat straddling the nose of a moose, facing its antlers and concentrating on freeing the hide from the skull. It was nearly dusk. Light snow was falling on the Alaskan tundra, and all was silent until he heard a slight rustle behind him. He shot a glance over his shoulder. A bush four feet to his rear was shaking, snow falling from its limbs.

"Birds must have flown from it," Jim thought as he turned back to his work. His friend, Charles Schreck, who was in his mid-sixties, had shot the moose, and they both had begun cutting and bagging the meat. The air, however, had become cold. Lucille, Charlie's wife, was shivering, so Jim loaded each of their backpacks with thirty pounds of meat and suggested they take the packs and the guns back to camp. He promised to fill his own backpack and be right behind them. But after the Schrecks left, he remembered that Charlie had decided to have the head mounted. Freeing the hide from the brow and between the antlers of a frozen head is difficult, so Jim decided to tackle that chore before packing more meat. Again, the bush rustled behind him. Jim looked, saw nothing, and once more concluded that it must be camp-robber birds searching for tidbits of meat.

He had just resumed skinning when his senses told him something was very wrong. He again glanced around. "Can't be birds," he thought. "There isn't a bird *anywhere*!" And *no* birds in the wild usually means a threatening presence.

Jim stood up and turned to see not the bush he expected, but a bear emerging on all fours, now just three feet away. The bear, surprised to see a man rise six feet seven inches out of what it regarded as free lunch, wheeled and ran.

Jim's sigh of relief had not yet escaped his lips when the bear—a grizzly from its coat and hump—wheeled around so fast that there was no time for him to react.

The charging bear hit Jim like a pickup truck, grabbing him by the right thigh and carrying him ten feet, shaking his whole 225 pounds, and bouncing his head on the ground the entire distance before throwing him into a tundra bowl. Jim landed sprawled on his back in this depression in the earth with arms outstretched and legs over the rim. The grizzly backed off ten feet and stopped next to the moose.

Thoughts raced through Jim's mind—even the thought that seeing your life flash before you at the moment of impending death is not a device of fiction. His wife, Judy, was at home in New York State. Would he ever see her again? What if he hadn't been raised in Colorado gold country? Would he have gotten interested in gold mining north of Fairbanks? Would he be in Alaska right now? What about Lee Peet, bush pilot and ex-partner in the mine until they sold out in 1986? Cold air was spitting the snow now. A storm was imminent. When would Lee be able to fly in? If Jim survived the bear, would Lee be in time to save him? How badly had the bear mangled his leg?

Jim didn't examine the leg. Books say don't move. Play dead when attacked by a bear. Maybe the bear will go about its business if it perceives no further threat.

What if he hadn't gotten interested in bow hunting? The Schrecks had the only guns, and they were on their way back to camp.

Charlie's moose had been down since 8:00 A.M. If only they hadn't decided to eat pancakes after field dressing the animal and returning to camp for meat sacks and backpacks. While the coffee perked, Jim had walked out to his tree stand in a spruce where he glassed for moose. And there had been one moose—one bull as big as he had ever seen.

Jim had told Charlie and Lucille about the animal, grabbed his Oneida Eagle bow, and rushed out to get closer. A mile from camp, he stalked within fifty yards of the bull. Too far—he would never risk a shot that might only wound an animal. The bull then vanished and Jim closed the distance. He could sense the animal was nearby, but he couldn't see a thing. He peered over a bush and, *whoops*, the bull was staring back from only fifteen yards away. But again, it slipped off into the scenery.

Twice more Jim managed to stalk within thirty yards of the elusive bull. But never could he get a good, clear, close shot. Sensibly, he decided to back off, let the bull relax, and make another try the next morning. By then, however, five hours had passed. Charlie's moose still needed to be skinned and quartered. And by the time they got some of the meat boned out, it was 6:00 P.M. Now he was sprawled in a tundra bowl with a multitude of thoughts flashing past in the brief seconds the bear stood indecisively looking back and forth from the moose to him.

Almost with disbelief, Jim noticed that he still had the skinning knife. It was Lucille's, a Smith & Wesson drop point with a three-and-three-quarter-inch fixed blade, honed to a shaving edge. Oddly, it was in his left hand, the blade pointing down from his grip. Perhaps he had been pulling the hide with his right hand and slashing along the skull with his left.

Jim didn't dare move, yet he knew he couldn't lie there very long. He was wet from being thrashed in the tundra. All he had on were jeans and a long-john top. His camouflage hunting jacket was lying on the ground out of reach. He hadn't needed its warmth while he worked on the moose. Now darkness was closing in fast, and he was becoming very cold. But he resolved to remain motionless as long as he could. If the bear looked away, he planned to roll into a fetal position, as the books also advise, to protect his belly. Mostly, he hoped the bear would begin eating moose meat and forget about him.

The grizzly once more looked longingly at the moose before turning back to Jim. This time he intuitively recognized that the bear's indecision was over. But there was no time to roll into a ball. In one bound, the grizzly landed on Jim's legs, instantly closing its jaws on his right knee.

Although severe, Jim's thigh wounds, due to shock, were not yet terribly painful. Nor were the new bites to the knee. And then one canine tooth hooked over his kneecap and entered the joint—probably hitting a nerve. Jim jerked upward in pure reaction, cursing loudly, and repeatedly stabbing the knife into the neck of the bear that was almost in his face.

The surprised grizzly jumped off and ran twenty yards. Jim made up his mind. He was finished with following advice. Playing dead had not worked. He was now operating on instinct, and every fiber was urging him to get the hell out of there. He struggled to his feet, but the bear was already charging back at him. Jaws open, all four of its canines drove into his left thigh before the momentum threw him back into the same tundra bowl. His legs flipped up as he fell, and the bear bit all the way through the back side of his left thigh.

Again, Jim lunged out with the knife, striking the same place on the right side of the neck because again the bear was in the same head-on position. The thrusts were hurting. The bear snapped at the fist that held the knife, bit through one finger, and left a row of tooth marks across the back of Jim's hand. But the bear bit the knife in the bargain. And the blade was pointing down into its tongue and lower jaw.

The Schrecks were two hundred yards down the trail toward camp when Charlie stopped abruptly. "Did you hear that?"

Lucille hadn't.

"I think a bear has Jim. He's cussing and calling for help!"

Charlie forgot the bellyband on his backpack and shrugged off the shoulder harness with such force that the weight of the meat threw him on his back like an upturned turtle. Lucille quickly helped free him, and Charlie took off in the dim light with his rifle—battling straight through the willows and low-growing whitethorn toward the sounds of Jim and the bear. He could not be sure that Jim would be on or even near the trail.

Jim kept yelling for Charlie and swearing at the bear. The grizzly growled, and several times Charlie heard another strange sound—a sort of *erk*. Was it the sound of teeth against bone? Or what Charlie couldn't know—the bear's responses to being stabbed? Perhaps even the bear gagging on the blood rushing from its tongue?

And then all noises of battle ceased. Charlie's fears escalated. Was Jim dead? With no sounds to guide him, he quickly cut across to the trail.

The battle had not stopped with the cessation of noise, however. The bear had simply run a second time from the sting of the knife. Jim had scrambled to his feet just in time to see the bear charging again on all fours from fifteen yards away. But this charge had lost ferocity. The grizzly was weakening either in strength or resolve. It simply ran up and clamped its teeth onto Jim's lower left leg, punching one tooth hole in his ten-inch leather boots and four in the flesh above.

Jim was now towering over the bear. He felt an exhilarating sensation of dominance. He pressed his advantage. He thrust the knife with all of his might, much improved by his upright position, once more into the right side of the grizzly's neck. Then he drew back his arm to stab again, but the knife was gone!

Had it stuck in bone? It had a checkered rubber handle that was no doubt partially responsible for staying in his grip throughout the thrashing he endured, but perhaps by now it had become slick with blood. Jim was desperate, even angry. He fully intended to kill that bear on the spot, and truly believed he could. He reached down and groped for the knife he felt was sticking in the bear. He grabbed a handhold of hair on the grizzly's hump so he could stabilize himself and reach lower.

Threats and punishment all come to a predator cub from above, and the memory stays with the adult. The bear let go of Jim's leg, jerked free of this threatening grip, and ran away the usual fifteen or twenty yards. This time, however, when the bear stopped, it stood facing away. Jim perceived this as the right moment to violate book advice once more. He ran, an act that usually invites chase. Despite his wounds, he ran to open tundra, and then walked twenty yards across the wet, grassy indentations to the trail the Schrecks had taken earlier. There he glanced back at the grizzly. It was standing on its hind legs watching.

Gut feeling told him that the bear had had quite enough of Jim Mariotte. And no intuition was necessary to know that Jim Mariotte had sure as hell had enough of the bear. Jim turned to leave, took three steps, and there was Charlie Schreck coming up the trail. "Jim! Was that a grizzly?"

"Sure was."

"Did he get you, Jim?"

"Sure did."

Charlie tried to help support Jim on his feet. "Did he hurt you bad?"

"Not good, Charlie, but nothing's broken. And I don't think he cut any important arteries."

Had they taken two steps back, Charlie could have shot the bear, but that was not the priority. "Let's get back to camp while I can still move," Jim said. "I'm too big and heavy to carry."

It was becoming quite dark now, but with the snow reflecting whatever light remained, it was possible to stay on the trail blazed with surveyor's tape. Jim found it faster to walk by himself rather than trying to lean on Charlie for support. In fact, at six feet seven inches, Jim's long legs soon outdistanced his older, shorter companion. He suddenly came upon the Schrecks' backpacks. But no Lucille. "Lucille!"

No answer. "LUCILLE!"

Still no answer. Jim yelled again at the top of lungs. At last, he got a response . . . from above! Lucille had dropped her pack, distanced herself from the potentially bear-attracting meat, and climbed to the top of a forty-foot spruce the moment Charlie left to help Jim. "I can't get down," she called. How a sixty-year-old woman got that far off the ground was a puzzle to the men, neither of whom was available to help at the moment. Jim had to keep moving. Lucille fought back her fears, tried, and made it down.

The Schrecks were asking numerous questions, but Jim put them off. "We'll talk about it in camp," he said. His greatest fear was losing consciousness on the trail. His friends would not be able to drag his heavy weight to camp if he went into shock. He had moved well at first, but now he could feel himself stiffening and slowing. It became harder and harder to lift his legs. Eventually, he was depending on the Schrecks to stay upright. As they neared camp, they were almost carrying him. At the tent, Jim couldn't lift his feet over the threshold. They dragged him inside.

Charlie lit a lantern and saw that Jim's jeans were covered with blood—some from the moose, much his own, and perhaps more from the bear. They stripped off the bloody garments, washed away the blood and dirt, gave Jim two of Lucille's arthritis pain pills, and poured whiskey into his wounds. Unfortunately, the first-aid kit was in Jim's pack, which was back at the attack site. Clean meat bags were all they had to wrap the wounds.

Suddenly, the cold air, aided by blood loss and evaporating whiskey, sent excruciating cramps into Jim's muscles. Jim grabbed Charlie, reached around him, and tried to pull out some of the painful knots in his upper body. "What the hell are you doing?!" Charlie demanded. Jim looked at his face and realized he was about to pop his friend's eyeballs out. He let go, and Charlie made ready his own sleeping bag because it unzipped all the way. They could roll Jim in or out as necessary.

Lucille hurriedly grabbed a clean pair of Charlie's thermal underwear, thinking they would be bigger around and could be pulled onto Jim more easily. It was not as simple as she imagined, but they somehow managed to get him inside them. With Jim zipped into Charlie's sleeping bag and another thrown over him, the cramping subsided as he warmed. Later, Lucille went looking for her own underwear, now strangely missing, and realized that they were the ones currently on Jim.

Pain pills every two hours got him through the night, but by morning, Jim's legs wouldn't bend. "Never mind," he thought, "someone will fly in today." But then Charlie pulled back the tent flap, and the magnitude of the blizzard that had hit the area could be seen. It was three days before Lee Peet could land and fly Jim the one hundred miles to a hospital in Fairbanks. The Schrecks watched as the plane, heavy with Jim and extra fuel, nipped the top of a tree as it labored in takeoff.

The next day, Lee flew back with two mutual friends to trail the bear. Charlie and Lucille lead them up the trail to the moose. No meat had been eaten. The grizzly had not cared to return, if, indeed, it was able. This was September 13, 1987, just four days after the attack. Despite the fact that recent rain and thawing had washed away much of the evidence, there was still ample blood to easily trail the bear. If it couldn't be seen on the tops or sides of bushes, the trackers would crawl through the brush where they could see blood on the undersides of leaves. The blood was head- and neck-high for a bear on all fours, verifying Jim's account of having stabbed the grizzly in the neck repeatedly.

The bear was trailed about three-eighths of a mile through a patch of short brush and across open tundra to higher and thicker growth. Here the trackers decided that it would not be prudent to follow. A wounded and, if alive, very angry bear would be extremely dangerous where visibility is but several feet at best.

Jim Mariotte and the Schrecks returned the next year. Charles Schreck had been stricken with cancer and wanted one more autumn hunt in Alaska.

He died that December. Jim has been back repeatedly and searches for the knife each time. He believes that the bear carried it off and died of the wounds. "You can't be afraid of bears," he said, "but you *must* respect them. You're in their country."

And that is what this book is all about. Bear attacks are multiplying because human activity is increasing our encounters with bears. Fear is not the answer. Neither is annihilating the bears. To be able to live with the bears without fear requires confidence born of experience and understanding. And some of that knowledge has carried a price too high to be ignored or forgotten.

THE GRIZZLY SKULL CRACKER

The huge bear dropped Ben Moore on his back and stood looking at his face. Ben might have played dead, but the desperateness of the situation was turning his terror into furor. Angrily, he brought both hands up toward the bear's open mouth, cocking his single action .357 Ruger on the way.

It was a clear autumn day with temperatures in the forties, but the thirty-five- to forty-five-mile-per-hour winds gave the air a sharp chill. There were no sizable trees to act as windbreaks, only brush and scrubby trees growing to five or six feet, so Ben Moore and his hunting buddy, Richard Napoleone, decided to glass the rolling hills for moose from the comfort of their Jeep. But they needed a better vantage point. A clearing about a hundred yards away looked promising. It was down the slope somewhat, but from it, the hunters might have excellent command of the draws between the fairly steep-sided fingers leading out from the hills.

"I'll walk down and check it out," Ben said, leaving his rifle in the Jeep. "I'll be right back."

Ben was aware that bears were in the area, so he did carry a .357 Magnum single-action Ruger. And he did try to avoid thickly grown brush wherever possible. When he had nearly reached the end of the forty-foot-wide and more than one-hundred-foot-long clearing, he was careful to stand in the open, away from the bushes, as he raised his binoculars to glass the countryside.

Not a moose was in view, but the area looked good. He swept the binoculars across the draws beyond one side of the clearing . . . then beyond and across the end . . . when, suddenly, the glass was filled with the image of a bear—and one so close to Ben that it was out of focus. The bear saw him at the same time, and as he dropped his binoculars, it stood up for a better look from above the bushes. For several seconds it stood staring, opening its mouth and bobbing its head, and then dropped from sight a hundred feet away and perhaps ten feet back in the vegetation.

Ben was somewhat startled, but not especially frightened. Knowing that most bears aren't looking for trouble, he stood perfectly still. The bear might wander off, or come closer for a look, but running away from it would only invite chase. Any other movement or sound might be regarded as a challenge. Moore was listening for sounds and glancing around for the bear's whereabouts when the huge animal burst from the bushes and charged across the clearing at full speed.

Ben was terrified, but with incredibly cool, rational thinking for a time like this, he recognized, just as his revolver cleared the holster, that the single-action is basically flawed for bear defense. If he raised his thumb to cock the hammer, he'd weaken his grip. If the bear hit him at that time, he'd very likely lose his firearm. He swiftly solved the problem by using his left hand to cock the hammer. He pulled the trigger just as the bear was five feet from the barrel.

The bullet slammed into its chest, but the grizzly showed no reaction. On the run, it grabbed Ben below the right knee, spun him over its head, and sent him flying several feet against a large rock.

Ben barely touched ground before the bear grabbed him again by the same leg. He fired once more, but was being shaken so severely that he missed the animal. A third time he managed to cock the .357 with his left hand. The bear's stomach was now a foot from his face, its teeth still attacking his leg. He fired, opening a huge gut wound. Blood gushed, and the bear spun around, enraged. It grabbed him by the head and shook. Ben could feel his skull crack around his eyes and cheekbones. His nose was hanging off to the side. Blood filled his left eye. And then the bear dropped him on his back.

The grizzly stood over Ben, looking down at his face, mouth open. Ben might have played dead, but the desperateness of the situation was turning his terror into furor. Angrily, he brought both hands up, cocking the Ruger on the way. The bear came down with its jaws to grab whatever was moving. Both of Ben's hands and the revolver with a six-inch barrel were all of the way in its mouth when, a split instant before it bit down, he pulled the trigger.

The grizzly recoiled, shuddering and shaking its head, then swung a powerful paw at the revolver, barely glancing Ben's gun hand, but leaving a sliver of claw stuck all of the way through his thumb. Incredibly, Ben still clung to his firearm.

Having no trouble staying on its feet, but seemingly disoriented, the bear walked slowly off into the bushes. Quickly, Ben tried to stand. He didn't want to be caught lying down if the bear returned. His right leg collapsed. He stood again, jamming his leg down hard to make it hold him. This time, it did.

Only one cartridge remained in the cylinder. Ben couldn't see through the blood streaming into his eyes well enough to reload, but his right hand found the ejection rod. The spent cases seemed glued into the cylinder by his coagulating blood, but three came out. He felt for the loading port and managed to slide two live cartridges into the chambers. The bear hadn't yet returned.

Now overcome by anger, nearly blinded, wiping his right eye, his left eye out of its socket, Ben stood shouting a profane challenge for the grizzly to come back and finish what it had started. But the bear had had enough.

Several minutes later, Richard started down the slope. He had heard just one of the shots over the noise of the wind.

"Did you get a moose?"

"No, a bear got me," Ben answered into the wind.

"What?"

"A bear got me," he yelled again, and by then Richard was close enough to see for himself. Shaken by the sight, he assisted his friend to the Jeep. He had driven no more than a hundred feet when the engine quit. Anxiously watching for the bear, Richard slid under the vehicle and pounded the electric fuel pump, which had been giving them trouble.

When the Jeep at last restarted, Richard tried to contact other members of their hunting party by CB radio. There was no answer, but two paramedics near camp heard the message and called ahead for help. Three more paramedics arrived in an ambulance.

Five hours and a torturous journey later, Ben arrived at Fairbanks Memorial Hospital, but facial reconstruction wouldn't begin until the shattered bones could mend. Six operations later, Ben's wife was able to joke that thanks to the bear her husband looks better now than he did before. "I just thank God," he said, "that there wasn't room for my son, Ty," then fourteen, "to ride with us in the Jeep." Ty instead went with two other friends in a station wagon. "Otherwise, he'd have been with me in that clearing, and he'd have been attacked as well."

Richard joined the Alaska Department of Fish and Game personnel in a helicopter search for the bear. It was never found, but a sow with two second-year cubs had been observed in the area three days earlier, and Richard did see two grown cubs leaving the area at a fast pace about four miles from the attack site. The sow may have thought that she was defending her cubs. Or she may have been guarding a gut pile. It was later learned that a moose had been killed near the clearing a couple of days prior to the attack.

"Most bears don't attack," Ben said, "and when they do, they usually have a reason. Unfortunately, we can't always know when they have that reason. And sometimes it's just temperament that makes an individual bear respond differently."

Human response to being bulldozed by bears can be equally unpredictable. Some quit hunting or move away from bear territory entirely. Others go on with their daily lives, almost as if nothing happened. Ben Moore hadn't hunted bears until one hunted him.

DEATH CAME CALLING

This man-eating grizzly defending its kill charged down the mountain and was one yard from a man firing a .30/30 when Don Kluting's shot tore through both of its shoulders. Instantly, the bear did a ninety and was two jumps from Don who remembers every fine detail as if it happened in slow motion. One other memory of this brave young man is etched with equal precision. Back at Port Alexander, a young girl slowly walked past the houses and into the woods along the beach. Someone said, "That's Harley's daughter," and they went to be with her.

Less than a city block up the heavily timbered slope, a man-eating bear was defending its kill. The bear had already roared its challenge. It had threatened with an eruption of short, brush-breaking false charges. But the man-eater couldn't be seen because it was up a slope of old growth spruce and western hemlock that stood eighty or ninety feet above an understory thick with blueberry bushes and saplings.

It was a doubly tense moment for Don Kluting and his six-man search-and-rescue team. Facing a killer bear ready to kill again, Don was with a team he hadn't asked for—and the team hadn't asked for him. The six men were untrained and poorly armed friends, as well as friends of friends, of the bear's victim. Don was a total stranger to them—and at twenty-two, a very young stranger at that—trying to take charge of a job that the rest of the group was pretty sure that they could do better on their own.

Don asked three of the six to stay on the vantage point of a ridge. The other three would go up the slope with him. His group had gone only fifteen feet when two of the three with him declined. In fact, they said, they would go farther back down the slope a distance. They felt that their rifles weren't heavy enough to be of value in a close encounter with an Alaska bear.

The third man, Jim Lange, who was the best armed of the three, not only volunteered, but he was also determined to go right now! He was carrying a .338-06, a necked-up version of the .30-06. Don had a .338 Winchester Magnum. The pair started up the hill slowly, quietly, hoping to get a clear shot at the bear before it saw them. An unidentified noise stopped the two before they got ten feet. Was the bear circling? They listened, and then moved on another few feet. At this point, they were less than thirty feet from the three men who remained on the ridge.

Suddenly, the bear rose on its hind legs and grunted, its head poking above the bushes for just a moment at about seventy yards. Then all hell broke loose. Crashing through the undergrowth, knocking over two-inch diameter saplings as easily as a running man might stomp down weeds, the giant bear charged all five men.

At first, Don and Jim could only see bushes whip and saplings fall. Then the bear became flashing brown blurs among the blueberries. At fifty yards, both men fired, each confident that he had hit the man-eater. But the bear charged on. "It's like throwing rocks at a freight train," Don thought as he desperately chambered another cartridge.

Two of the three men on the ridge then fired their rifles. The third stepped backward, tumbled, and found himself hanging over a fifteen-foot drop-off. One rifle jammed after the first shot. The man with the .30/30 fired again.

The charging bear glanced toward Don and Jim as if intending to attack them first, then at twenty yards swerved toward the group on the ridge, probably because the .30/30 had stung it in the foot.

Don's rifle was set up for deer and goat hunting with a Leupold 3X-to-9X variable scope. There hadn't been time to remove the eyepiece, and Don had difficulty keeping the bear in his sights. Everything was too magnified, even though the power had been adjusted down to 3X. He picked up the bear's head in the scope, and then swung to the front to establish a lead, keeping part of the head in the left edge of the glass. Both he and Jim were trying for shoulder shots that would break the bear down and put it on the ground where it could be finished off. Only a brain or spine shot would have killed it instantly, and both men knew that those are terribly small targets to hit on a bear running broadside. A heart or lung shot would have been useless. The bear would have had time to kill all of them before it died. A bear can run another one hundred yards after a heart shot, even farther after a lung shot.

Jim fired. Don saw the bear flinch. Don then fired again, just as he could see the orange muzzle blast of the .30/30 flash in the right-hand edge of his scope. It wasn't that he fired quickly because there was no more room to continue leading the bear; pulling the trigger and seeing the flash in his scope were simply simultaneous events. But the horror of the situation drained through his body. The bear was perhaps a yard off the end of the .30/30 barrel—a fraction of a jump from the three men. Although Don automatically began chambering another cartridge, he knew that there was no way for either he or Jim to get off another shot before the bear killed or badly mauled all three men. Furthermore, they were only twenty feet from the bear themselves. If they couldn't break the bear's shoulders or hit the brain or spine, they'd be the killer's next victims.

All of this had started very pleasantly. Forty-three-year-old Harley Sievenpiper Jr. of Juneau, Alaska, had been engaged in one of his life's greatest pleasures—his annual deer hunt with old friends. Harley had joined Jim Hendricks and Dave Traygo, residents of Port Alexander on Baranof Island, and the trio had motored a fishing boat down the coast to a bay called Port Conclusion. It was only a forty-five-minute trip, so the three had planned to hunt the day, and then return to the anchored boat and sail back to Port Alexander for the night.

Harley told his friends that he planned to use a deer call that sounded like the bleat of a distressed fawn. He would hunt the edges of muskegs where visibility would be better than among the blueberries and tall evergreens. A few bull pines and cedars grow in these areas, but muskegs are mostly open, with thick moss and potholes up to fifteen feet deep spotted here and there. A Sitka blacktail deer coming to a call in a muskeg would make for a relatively easy shot. The three hunters then scattered about two hundred yards apart.

Around 1:30 P.M., Jim Hendricks heard a bear roar, followed by Harley's scream. Hendricks fired three shots to call Dave Traygo, and the two immediately went to investigate. Walking in the direction from which the sounds had come, the two found the attack site within ten minutes, but the hopelessness of the situation was all too evident. Being experienced hunters, Hendricks and Traygo recognized that Harley couldn't have survived losing the amount of blood that covered much of the violently torn-up area. Harley's body had been taken, and this made the situation even more dangerous. If they encountered the bear, it would try to defend its kill. They also didn't know if they could deal with the sight of what had happened to their close friend. They decided to go for professional help.

When they returned to Port Alexander, Hendricks called Ketchikan. No, they told him, they couldn't handle it, but he might try calling Petersburg or Wrangell. Neither of those towns would provide help, either, so Hendricks called Juneau. No, they said, call Sitka. Hendricks finally reached Fish and Wildlife Protection Officer Roland Young, and yes, indeed, Young told him, jurisdiction and responsibility did rest in Sitka. By that time, however, all of the residents of the tiny fishing village of Port Alexander had become highly agitated by what they perceived as a runaround. They concluded that, one way or another, they'd have to take the matter into their own hands.

Back in Sitka, Officer Young called Don Kluting for assistance. Don had helped him in cases of wildlife violations, so he trusted his professionalism. Don worked for the city of Sitka, was a volunteer EMT (emergency medical technician) on the ambulance, belonged to the volunteer fire department, had been trained in both tracking and search-and-rescue field management, and had already demonstrated his abilities in a number of search-and-rescue operations.

As the Bet-Air floatplane slowed and lost altitude to land them at Port Conclusion at about 8:00 A.M. the next day, the two men glanced at each other with concern. Two fishing boats at anchor in the bay below had only one man watching over both. As feared, a dozen Port Alexander residents, resentful of what they thought was bureaucratic indifference and unnecessary delay, had taken off on their own. And twelve men milling around on a trail can obliterate a whole lot of evidence in moments.

"Can the group be reached by marine radio?" Young had asked. The watchman affirmed that the group had a portable unit with them. "Okay," Young said, "let's call and tell them to stay put until we catch up."

Harley's day-old footprints in the mud of a worn, well-traveled trail led them to the second muskeg, about two hundred yards from the beach. Don spotted a blue fanny pack. It was the attack site.

Harley's glasses, gloves, hat, lighter, watch, and pack were scattered about on the bloody, torn-up vegetation. Apparently, he had been positioned behind an old stump, blowing his deer call and watching the muskeg. His Ruger .300 Winchester Magnum rifle was driven at a 45-degree angle through the deep moss and into the stump by the impact of the bear. Only inches of the shoulder stock remained visible above the moss. The muzzle was embedded so deeply into the partially rotted stump that it required both hands of both men to pull it free.

Fortunately, the search party hadn't found the site and stomped out the signs. Don was able to read that the bear had come running (the prints in crushed moss and in the dirt below were far apart) down a fifteen-foot high hump of ground directly behind its victim. Harley probably never knew of the bear's presence until it hit him. His rifle had remained on safety, the scope covers had been removed, and a cartridge was in the chamber with three more in the magazine.

The drag trail going away from the site and up the slope was easy for the pair to follow. It was evident that for a time the bear had dragged Harley by the shirt. When a piece of the shirt had torn off, the bear had spit it out and taken a new grip.

Within a hundred yards, they caught up with the search party. The group's tone was openly hostile. Four-letter words flew freely, as the more vocal members made it clear that they weren't out there to take orders from anybody. They had missed the first seventy-five yards of the drag but had followed the trail another twenty-five yards after discovering a boot and bits of cloth.

Trailing is slow, tedious work, and Young immediately recognized that fourteen men couldn't do it together. While Don would be patiently searching for minute clues, the others would, no doubt, be impatiently walking ahead of him, blotting out the signs. In addition, the extra twelve men were armed—most not well enough to challenge a grizzly, but all well enough to do each other harm. Young cut the problem in half by asking six men to go with Don and the other six to accompany him. He would stay behind a hundred yards or more to be out of the way while Don tracked.

Nevertheless, Don had problems. Six men are still too many to control when you're concentrating on tracking, especially when those men don't believe that you know what to look for, anyhow. To compound the problem, unbeknownst to Young, two of the men he sent with Don had been drinking.

Finally, Don found a splinter of bone, and some of his team began to exhibit greater confidence in his ability. He radioed Young, who then caught up to photograph and collect the sliver. Trust continued to build as Don found other bits of flesh and bone, but the sight of these body parts also made everyone increasingly nervous.

Each time thereafter that a squirrel darted or a bird flew, safeties had clicked and three or four rifles jumped to shoulders. "Okay, guys, calm down a bit." Don had to give his speech over and over. "Think straight. Don't try to shoot at everything that moves, or we'll get someone shot out here."

Bits of evidence were scattered for more than a mile. The farther the group trailed, the more serious and dangerous the situation became. Many bears leave their victims at the attack sites, and 70 percent of those people survive. If a bear claims its kill, it'll usually drag the body two hundred or three hundred yards at most and cover the remains with brush and other vegetation. Some victims have survived being covered and left behind. Seldom do searchers who arrive on the scene see the bear, and neither Officer Young nor Don had expected to see this one. Don brought along his rifle, just to be sure, but Young carried only the medical supplies they would need to stabilize Harley if he was found alive—and a body bag if he wasn't.

On and on the team trailed until they were seventeen hundred feet above the bay and a mile and a half from the attack site—an incredible distance for a bear to drag its kill. Don gave his stay-calm speech one last time, and then began to have his own strange feelings. "Guys, it's just something in my guts, but I think we're close."

Somebody laughed. "Now who's nervous?"

No more pieces of flesh or bone were found for two hundred yards, but the team remained controlled, staying behind as Don slowly searched his way from one little piece of overturned moss to the next. About a hundred yards beyond where he had his gut feeling, he thought that he heard something and stopped the team. Nothing more. He then whistled, and that was when the silence was shattered by the enormity of the unseen giant's roar, huffing challenge, and brush-breaking short false charges.

Don radioed Young. "The bear is close. We can't see it, but it's just up the slope. And it's threatening. What do you want us to do?"

"If you get a good shot, put it down," Young radioed back. "The main thing is, concentrate on getting that good shot. A wounded bear could be a disaster."

Don had never before killed a bear. He had hunted with his father since age eight and had hunted deer by himself since fourteen. He had gotten bear tags for six years to avoid having to surrender the hide to the state in case he did have to kill one, but shooting a bear hadn't been a desire of his. So far, he had been successful in chasing off curious bears by shooting close to them.

Nevertheless, Don then split his team and confidently started up the slope with Jim Lange. Rifle-handling had become practiced second nature, and adrenaline was perhaps making both men steadier and surer of themselves than they had any right to be.

This bear's behavior had already proved bizarre when the animal attacked Harley, who didn't have a deer to steal and who wasn't exposing the odors of meat and blood to the air (which is usually what attracts a grizzly to a hunter). It had continued to act strangely when it had dragged its victim a mile and a half instead of the usual couple of hundred yards. And the bear compounded the unexpected when it raged down the slope to attack five men—seven, if it had known that there were two others thirty or forty yards below.

The charging bear had showed no response to Don's and Jim's shots at fifty yards. Jim's next shot had caused a flinch, and Don had triggered his second shot just as the bear was in the faces of the three men on the ridge. Don then reached for the bolt on his Ruger M-77 with the full knowledge that there was no more that he could do to protect his team. Even if the bear died at that instant, its momentum alone would carry it into those men with the impact of a car going thirty-five miles an hour. And bears—assuming that this one was hit at all—do not die instantly from shoulder wounds.

At the precise moment that Don reached for his bolt, the bear, in its most unpredictable move of all, changed its mind about killing the three men just a step away. Don saw its head swing toward him and Jim with its teeth bared and an unmistakable message issuing from the raging hate in its eyes: "You are the ones hurting me; you will die."

Don was seeing and registering every little detail as if things were happening in slow motion. The bear pivoted on its right leg. The left leg came around the right one as the bear executed its sudden 90-degree turn. Don's bolt had not yet quite ejected the empty case. The bear was now two jumps away, when once again, this time not through choice, it did the unexpected. Its right front leg was collapsing. Downhill momentum rolled the bear's front end onto its left shoulder while its rear end twisted until both hind legs were straight up—for just a moment. Then the hind legs flopped down, too, leaving the whole bear on its left side. But through it all, the bear's head remained level, angry eyes fixed on Don and Jim.

Movement forty feet up the slope caught Don's eye. Everything had happened so fast that a skinny, dead sapling thirty feet tall and five inches in diameter was still in the process of falling after the bear was down.

The man with the .30/30—psychologically frozen into a split-second earlier time—was still firing up the hill. The bear had been just off the end of his rifle barrel. Someone shouted, and he stopped.

Don finished chambering a live cartridge and quickly moved to his right to take the three men on the ridge more safely out of the line of fire. Stepping on a log to gain better elevation for a more effective head shot, Don fired at the bear, hitting it and extinguishing the rage from its eyes.

"What's going on? Is everyone all right?" Officer Young was radioing urgently. "We heard shooting."

"All okay," Don radioed back. "The bear is dead. But now that it's over, I'm shaking so badly I can't stand up. The bear was so close to three of our men that I'm amazed they aren't dead from heart attacks."

The two men down the slope had only seen bushes whip and heard gunfire, so they weren't as shaken as everyone else. They had been Harley's close friends, and both immediately hurried up the hill to see if he was there and possibly alive. One of them yelled to say that they'd found him, but everyone knew from the tone of his voice that Harley was dead—and worse.

"Come back down," Don yelled. "Don't touch anything."

When the second group caught up, Young got the Port Alexander people started on skinning the bear, and then he and Don went up to retrieve Harley's body. Young rolled what was left of him into the bag using only peripheral vision. Don made the mistake of looking directly at the badly eaten remains.

Today, although the mind protects itself with forgetfulness, the details of that horrific sight are still etched in Don's memory with the same slow-motion, fine-grained accuracy with which he recalls the bear's charge. One more detail emerges with that kind of clarity. "We had just gotten back to Port Alexander in the fishing boats," he said. "I remember seeing a girl, maybe bordering on or just into her teens, walking away down the only road in town—out past the end of the houses and into the woods along the beach. Someone said, 'That's Harley's daughter,' and they went to be with her."

Harley Sievenpiper was the seventeenth person to be eaten by a bear this century. He had been the first in twelve years. His killer took six bullets. A .30/30 bullet had hit one of its feet as the bear charged directly at the shooter. One of either Don's or Jim's first shots at fifty yards had struck the chest cavity, possibly hitting the heart. The other had hit just behind the rib cage. Jim's second shot had broken the bear's right shoulder and gone halfway through its body. Lead from Don's .338 Magnum further shattered the bear's right shoulder, broke the left shoulder, and was later found emerging from the hide and hung up in the hair. The head shot was the sixth.

Although Officer Young and Don offered with some trepidation, Mrs. Sievenpiper declined hearing more of the details. She requested and would have cherished her husband's wedding ring, but it was never recovered. Neither were the deer call nor Harley's wallet, and perhaps other unknown personal items.

Don was subsequently presented with the State of Alaska's Medal of Bravery plus a $600 bonus from the City of Sitka's Honor Board for risking his life in the service of others.

Considerable controversy over what prompts bears to attack hunters continues to spark debate between groups of Alaska's hunters and biologists, with some of each arguing on both sides. There are those who claim that all bears are programmed to function as all bears function, and that they are motivated to attack only by smelling or seeing what they consider to be food. This group denies that bears are called to dinner by the reports of firearms or that they would be attracted by deer calls. Others believe that it is naive to think that individuals of a species as intelligent as the grizzly would be unable to learn new clues to finding easy meals. This group not only believes that some bears learn to respond to hunters' sounds, but that sows, in turn, pass on this knowledge to their cubs.

"It has become a definite problem in my area," Don said. "The salmon runs have been poor the last couple of years during August and September, when the bears should be laying on fat. Maybe the bears are forced to hunt deer instead. Drew Mathews, a member of our search-and-rescue team, was hunting along a hiking trail with a partner when a sow with cubs came running to his deer call. The two men yelled, and the bears stopped, but they wouldn't go away. They circled the hunters for an hour. Every time the men tried to leave, the sow would head them off. Finally, the men tried to run. The sow was right behind them. Drew's buddy fired a warning shot, and the bear took off. The men ran another quarter mile, looked around and there was the bear again. This time, another warning shot chased her off for good."

In October 1988, one month before Harley Sievenpiper was attacked, Don was hunting mountain goats above Katlian Bay and killed his animal at about thirty-one hundred feet. Ten minutes later, just as he had gotten to his goat, he saw a bear coming from a half mile away. The bear kept coming, so he fired a warning shot. Several shots later, the bear finally stopped at a small group of trees four hundred yards below. All the while Don boned meat off the skeleton, the bear paced back and forth in the trees, occasionally stepping out tentatively, but going back when the hunter yelled.

When he finished packing the meat, Don threw the goat remains over a drop-off and walked up the slope away from the bear. Although bears are supposed to have poor eyesight, this one obviously knew what Don had done and immediately trotted toward the carcass. Don slipped off the safety and raised his rifle in case the bear ran past the goat, but it didn't.

"This bear came to the sound of my rifle shot," he said. "Even if it could have smelled blood over a half mile away, air currents couldn't have conveyed the message that quickly. In fact, any air movement that day was in the wrong direction. There was no wind, and it was hot. Heat causes updrafts, and this bear was down the slope.

"That bear was hungry. And the bear that killed Harley Sievenpiper was hungry, as it had very little fat for a bear in early November. I'll let the experts argue whether certain individual bears have learned to correlate gunfire and deer calls with free lunch. But I've seen and heard enough to conclude that it's wise to hunt in pairs and to watch each other's backsides when calling deer or when field dressing any kind of animal in grizzly country."

BULLDOZER BEAR

With no weapon and only his backpack to take some of the punishment, Fred "Sky" Roberts's only hope for survival was his will to take the pain and convincingly play dead until the bear believed it.

Fred "Sky" Roberts stopped, startled by the sounds of something big walking in the leaves. Was it really as big as it sounded, or was it just a fox trotting in the vegetation? It was October 31, and it was a very dry Halloween on Kodiak Island, with most of the leaves fallen from the short alder bushes. The four- to five-foot-high grass still stood, but with the fifteen- to twenty-mile-per-hour wind, even the grass contributed to the sound on the brittle ten-degree day.

No, they weren't the quick *tick-tick* steps of a short-legged fox. This animal had to be bigger. Its steps sounded too far apart. The sound was getting louder, coming closer. Now the animal was running, and it was clearly much heavier than a deer.

At forty feet, a huge Alaska brown bear burst into view, crashing through the brush like a bulldozer, head low and thrust forward, bucket-mouth open for business.

All of this transpired within a span of a few seconds, and Sky knew that the bear would cover those last forty feet in less than a second. Bears run as fast as quarter horses, and thirty miles per hour is forty-four feet per second. Sky faced the charge defenselessly. There was nothing taller than a two-foot alder to climb, even if there had been time for that. He'd left his rifle with his friends.

All of this had started with Sky (so nicknamed because he had lived in the big sky country of Montana) assisting master guide Joe Hendricks in guiding a California client on a Kodiak bear hunt. Winds of fifty to sixty knots had kept them weathered in at the town of Kodiak, delaying the hunt for several days. When at last they could be air-taxied, Joe and the client had flown first, anxious to get started. Sky had followed with camp gear on the second flight and had unpacked on the shore of a six-mile-long lake.

Nothing had been seen while hunting on foot, so the men decided to use their inflatable boat to drift the shoreline and glass the mountainside for bears. Again they had sighted no bears, so Joe and the client decided to hunt for deer instead. The Sitka blacktail season concurred with bear season in the area, and because blacktails are found only in the coastal regions of the far North, they provide attractive bonus trophies for nonresident hunters. Sky had stayed behind to correct a minor problem the group had been having with their small outboard engine.

Two hours later, Sky tried to join his friends, but he hadn't found them at the rendezvous point. Another hour and a half later, he spotted them on the lower end of the long hill. They had met him halfway, anxious for the lunches he was carrying.

"We just killed a nice deer," Joe had said as he grabbed a sandwich and pointed. "Right after we eat, you pack it out, and we'll go hunting."

Sky had then emptied his pack and left his rifle behind. There would be more than a hundred pounds of meat, cape, and hide to carry, so he had tried to shed all of the extra weight that he could.

Sky was within seventy-five yards of the deer when he had heard the bear running in the leaves. The sow had either heard or smelled him. There had been no false charges or feints to bluff him off. She was defending the kill that she now considered hers, and she was charging straight in to do violent business with the intruder.

Instinctively, Sky raised an arm to defend his head, but the bear grabbed it on the run, jerking him off his feet, shaking him as a dog would to kill a rat. With a flip of her head, the sow slammed him to the ground, picked him up again by the backpack, and threw him several feet. She clamped onto his hip and tossed him straight up. The moment he struck earth, she had him again. Five times she threw him four or five feet away or straight up, twice by the backpack, and once each by the arm, leg, and hip.

On the last throw, Sky landed in a small depression in the ground. Pulling his legs up in a fetal position to protect his more vulnerable underside, he tried to play dead. Unconvinced, the bear bit at his back, legs, and backpack for what seemed nearly two minutes. Luckily, the backpack was easiest to grab, and thus took most of the punishment. Sky's eyes were already swelling from being slammed to the ground, and his back was to the bear, so he didn't know where she went when she backed off for perhaps ten seconds to watch for signs of life. Sky continued to play dead, but still unsatisfied, the bear bit at his head. Luckily, the force of the bite was lessened somewhat because the sow got the metal backpack extensions in her mouth along with Sky's skull. Nevertheless, she laid open part of his face, piercing an eyelid and pulling a flap of skin over that eye.

At last, he heard retreating steps, and gingerly turned his head to look. Through the thin slit of the barely open lid of his best eye, he saw the sow, accompanied by two yearling cubs, heading back toward the deer kill.

Joe and the client had been on the other side of the ridge nearly a hundred yards away and hadn't heard a thing. Badly mauled and almost blinded, Sky then struggled up the hill and yelled for attention.

Joe returned and helped him stay on his feet as he hobbled the nearly two miles back to the camp, but it was still well after dark by the time they reached their destination. Because of this, Sky had to suffer his wounds through the night before an aircraft could be signaled with a bright orange cross of sleeping pads placed on the beach. The Coast Guard then sent a medivac by helicopter and flew Sky to the hospital in the town of Kodiak.

"She was what we call a nine-foot bear," he said later. "Her hide would have squared and stretched to nine feet. As a professional hunter, I would have guessed her skull at twenty-seven to twenty-eight inches. She stood about five feet tall on all fours and probably seven and a half feet on her hind legs."

Sky Roberts no longer guides, but he still hunts.

ONE HUNTER'S DEATHLY PREMONITION

When Duane Christensen's premonition came true, only his partner's skill and super-calm determination could save him. Bill Burgess saw the bear's head rearing above the alders as it repeatedly pounced on Duane's back. Knowing the limits of his .270, it would have to be an offhand shot in the ear at eighty yards when the head paused between going up and down.

Duane Christensen felt uneasy as he drove to Anchorage, Alaska. He had, in fact, been feeling uneasy for two weeks. "This is crazy," he thought. "Seven old friends getting together to hunt deer, and I don't want to go! I have never not wanted to go hunting."

At Bill Burgess's home, where some of the hunters were meeting before the flight to Kodiak Island, his apprehension mounted. But he couldn't put his finger on it. Nor could he put it out of his mind. Finally, he tried to put it into words. "I don't think I should go on this hunt," he said.

His friends were astonished.

"Why?" they asked.

"Well, maybe I can't really afford it," Duane said.

He knew he was kidding himself.

Finances had never gotten in the way of a hunt before. He had always made do somehow. But the vague premonition wouldn't leave him. He called his wife, Lori, back in Fairbanks. She knew about his misgivings. "I'm canceling out," he said. "Thought I'd let you know I'm driving back."

Lori knew of her husband's love for hunting. She thought that later on he'd regret not going. Unselfishly, Lori convinced Duane that he ought to make the trip. Surely, the misgivings were only his imagination.

The next day, Duane and his companions flew to Kodiak. They chartered plane flights to Uganik Lake, rented a small cabin, and pitched a wall tent to accommodate their extra numbers.

It was the last Saturday in October, a bright, beautiful day. Duane, Bill, and another friend did a little hunting that afternoon, and Bill shot a deer. Duane puzzled over why he wasn't having fun. Ordinarily, hunting Sitka blacktails on Kodiak Island with his buddies put him on top of the world.

Everyone went his own way on Sunday. Deer density is high on Kodiak, so hunting was easy. A couple of the island's two thousand enormous brown bears were also spotted, but at long distance. Bill got his second deer, and hurt his bum knee while packing out the animal. He vowed to make shorter excursions from then on, but planned to shoot two more blacktails.

Duane killed a deer, but his customary enthusiasm for the hunt still eluded him.

On Monday morning, Duane and Bill took the skiff to the far side of the lake. Working their way up to a pass, they encountered a sow brown bear with cubs, but there was no trouble. Duane didn't expect any, either. He'd grown up where brown bears are abundant, on Chichagof Island, in southeastern coastal Alaska. He learned to hunt around bears during his early years. Even when he'd finally been false-charged by a grizzly up at Coldfoot in the Brooks Range, he'd waved, yelled, and stopped the sow at fifteen feet.

At thirty-eight, from long experience, Duane was conditioned to believe that bears are not serious threats—if you know what you're doing. Treat them with great respect. Make noise. Show them you're a human. Avoid them, if possible, especially sows with cubs.

After the pair separated to hunt their own chosen places, Bill encountered another bear. Though not feeling in danger, he climbed a tree to avoid even the possibility of a confrontation. Soon afterward, while still perched on a limb, he shot a big buck under his tree. And shortly after that, a second bear wandered out into the open, eighty or ninety yards away. He still didn't feel threatened, but he nevertheless was relieved when he had dragged his buck down to the beach.

Meanwhile, Duane, who also has a bad knee, strained the old injury, adding physical pain to his feeling of foreboding.

On Tuesday, Steve Adamczak shot a deer in terrain where dragging was difficult, so he boned out the meat and packed it to camp. Noticing that his knife was missing, he went back Wednesday morning to retrieve it at the kill site. The carcass was gone, the grass and weeds were licked clean of blood, and the knife was buried under debris.

That afternoon, Steve stalked slowly into a hillside clearing, looking and listening carefully for deer. Suddenly, he heard something jump back in the bushes. His eyes darted in that direction, looking for the deer he had visions of, but what he saw instead was an eight-hundred-pound brown bear running straight at him. Steve was startled, but hoped that the bear would stop instead of crossing an alder-studded swale that somewhat blocked its way. When the bear didn't even slow, he was alarmed. At thirty yards, he fired a warning shot into the dirt with his .270 Winchester. The bear pulled up at twenty-five yards, and then stood, swinging its head from side to side growling.

Steve growled back. It was as if his throat wouldn't do anything else. He was horrified, knowing that growling a challenge was *exactly* the wrong thing to do. He stepped backward, trying to add distance, realizing that the chances of aiming at, firing at, and dropping a close-up brown with a .270 are slim at best.

To Steve's amazement, the brown suddenly dropped to all fours and stepped backward five or ten yards into the alders and willows. But then it started to follow the brush-line cover to get downwind and figure out just what the hunter was. Feeling like an entree on a menu, he again decided on a course of action that invites attack. He ran—straight downhill through the brush in the direction of safer country. On brief stops to listen, he could hear the bear crashing through the brush. The bear followed Steve for more than a half mile. Fortunately, the bear must have been more curious than angry or hungry, because it could have overtaken him at any time.

Back at camp that night, his recounting of the experience sparked serious discussion of increased bear movement. Nearly everyone who had taken deer had noticed the disappearance of gut piles by the next day. From distant bear sightings early in the hunt, activity had escalated to what appeared to be close-up and conscious bear participation in the daily deer harvest.

The group decided that no one would hunt alone for the remainder of their week on the island. Duane agreed with the precaution, but felt no greater fear of bears than he had before. What continued to bother him was his strange feeling of impending disaster.

Both being slowed by gimpy knees, Duane and Bill paired for the Thursday hunt. That morning, one deer was shot and field dressed about a mile and a quarter from the cabin. The men hunted a little farther, stopped to eat lunch, and then decided to investigate a small hill before turning back to drag out their deer. Duane walked around one side, Bill the other.

Bill killed another deer and heard a bear *woof* immediately after his two shots. It was difficult to tell the direction, and impossible to gauge the distance. Duane heard the shooting and hurried around to help. Bill was uphill from Duane, so it was convenient to direct Duane to the kill from that vantage point. He could also stand guard should the bear emerge. Duane dragged the deer out of a band of alders and into a large grassy meadow so that nothing could sneak up unseen during the field-dressing process.

Joining Duane, Bill mentioned hearing the bear.

"Well, in that case," Duane said, "maybe I'll walk a little distance away and stand watch."

"Why not watch from above the band of alders?" Bill suggested. "That's only about forty yards away, and you might get a chance at another deer."

Duane had barely squeezed through the thick alder bushes when he saw a deer walking toward him. After the shot, the deer ran another forty yards, leaving a traceable blood trail. Duane angled through a second band of alders and came out right where the blacktail lay on the lower grassy edge of the hill's bald knob.

Bill heard the shot and watched until Duane found his deer. Knowing that his partner would be about eighty yards away, he returned to field dressing. Seconds later he heard a threatening roar. Bill dropped his knife, grabbed his rifle, and jumped back. If a bear was coming, he didn't want to be close to the deer. Seeing no bear, he glanced up toward his buddy. And there was a sow charging Duane. She was out of sight behind the alders before Bill could shoulder his rifle.

Duane was bent over his own deer when the bear roared. He, too, jumped up, holding his rifle in his left hand. He immediately saw the brown, and waved and yelled so that she would identify him as a human. She was now thirty-five yards away and showing no hesitation in her charge. Duane swung the rifle around to his right hand, fully intending to fire a warning shot. But in the quick moment it took to get his finger on the trigger, she had closed to fifteen feet. This was no false charge. There wasn't even time to shoulder the gun. Looking into the bear's eyes, Duane fired instinctively from the hip. The bear didn't flinch.

Duane stiffened against the impact and tried to shove the rifle muzzle into her mouth when she leaped. He missed. The sow hit the barrel with her chin, the force of her momentum knocking him onto his back. But his grip on the rifle was so tight that the muzzle stayed jammed under the bear's chin. The brown stood looking down at Duane, her head rolling from side to side against the gun's muzzle as she tried to get her jaws off the barrel and on the man.

There was time for one thought. "Bill will shoot, and it will all be over." But Bill could see only obscured movement behind the alders. He couldn't distinguish features. Shooting was too risky. Duane's hope of a quick resolution ended when the bear swatted the rifle out of his hands so fast he couldn't tell which paw she had used. He thought the gun had been knocked downhill, but it had instead flown uphill.

Duane was almost as fast. Before the bear's teeth could reach him, he spun onto his belly to protect his vulnerable underside. He managed to get his left hand around to somewhat defend his head and neck.

The sow bit into the back of Duane's right thigh, picked him up, and shook. Almost as quickly, she dropped him. She bit again, this time in the right buttock, and with more ferocity than before. Once more she shook Duane, but never did she raise her head high enough for Bill to see a safe target. Bill could only see brown movement and hear roaring. Again, the bear dropped Duane.

It's doubtful that Duane's bulk—even at six feet three inches and 235 pounds—was difficult for the bear to raise and shake, but unknown to Duane, he had shot the sow behind the right eye, not far from the hinge of her jaw. The 225-grain hand-load had not penetrated the skull, but had probably torn through jaw muscles and ranged into the neck. Perhaps it was painful for the sow to grip and shake, but whatever the cause, she changed tactics. Rearing up, she then pounced down onto Duane's lower back, raking outward with her claws.

Bill saw the bear's head and shoulders bob above the alders, but the sow dropped before he could raise his rifle. She repeated the raking pounce a little higher up Duane's back. Again her head was up and gone too quickly for a shot.

Bill was ready when the bear's head bobbed up the third time. Although he was shooting a .270, which can't be considered an effective brown bear caliber, his familiarity with his Winchester Model 70 Featherweight had made him a very effective offhand shot, even at eighty yards. The head came up broadside, facing to his left, and Bill sought the bear's ear with the crosshairs. When she paused momentarily between coming up and going down, he pulled the trigger. The impact of the bullet drove the head away, spinning her in a full circle before she crumpled to the ground five or six feet from Duane.

Duane turned his head, looking for his rifle. He couldn't see it. The bear *seemed* dead; there were no sounds of breathing. And then the breathing resumed—very raspy, but it was breathing. Duane's eyes shot back at the bear. She seemed to be looking straight at him. He averted his eyes to avoid a direct challenging stare that might motivate her to rise. But he couldn't hold back a yell. "She's breathing, Bill! Hurry!"

Bill was rapidly moving uphill in a slightly circuitous route that would bring him into the open a respectable distance from the bear.

When Bill had another open shot at the sow, she was not moving. But he took no chances. He shot her through the head three more times with his .270, then got Duane's .338 Winchester Magnum and shot her through the shoulders.

"Duane?"

"Yeah?"

"If you can move, crawl out from under that bush so I can look you over."

Duane crawled out. A claw slash near Duane's belt line was the deepest and most worrisome. The claw had stopped just short of cutting the intestinal liner. Bill knifed off Duane's undershirt and bound the wound. Gashes and tears were seeping, but not bleeding heavily. No air from the body cavity was coming out of any of the cuts; perhaps nothing vital had been punctured. But there was no way that Bill, at five feet ten inches, 170 pounds, could carry a man the size of Duane. "Can you stand?"

Duane struggled to his feet. Encouraged by his partner's rational responses and ability to move, Bill started him down the easiest route—a bear trail—to the lake. Two other companions who had been hunting a thousand yards away joined them. They helped Duane while Bill scouted ahead as a precaution against other bears.

Just before they got to the lake, a plane landed to deliver hunters to a guide's camp. What luck! Instant rescue! But the plane took off again before the men could reach the shore.

Duane was transported by skiff to camp, where Bill boiled water and cleaned the wounds. Bill used Vaseline-soaked bandages so that they wouldn't stick to the flesh. Unfortunately, the group had brought along no bleach or other disinfectant, and bacteria from the mouth of a bear are a serious threat.

As is so often the case, planes flying over couldn't be summoned. Bill is a pilot himself, so he took great care to discharge flares when the planes would be within range and the sun wouldn't be in the pilots' eyes. But it was no use.

Two days later, the charter pilot flew in for the scheduled pickup.

Duane was subsequently flown to Fairbanks Memorial Hospital, where Dr. William Wennen stitched up five feet of rips and cuts.

Will the group hunt deer on Kodiak Island again?

"We have a hunt already planned," Bill said. "You don't quit driving because you have an accident. You become more careful. Our experience will change the way we hunt, of course, and we hope our story will help others avoid further bear maulings.

"We will hunt in pairs. One will field dress in the open while the other guards from thirty or forty yards away. Standing together could get two hunters wiped out in one charge. And we won't repeat the mistake of getting eighty yards apart and dividing our attention during field dressing. A radio device to signal planes is a must, and someone needs to develop a list of first-aid supplies that are adequate for bear bites. We need to be better prepared."

Duane Christensen also had one more comment: never again will he ignore a persistent premonition under dangerous circumstances.

DEVIL'S CLUB BEAR

Yelling could and did bring the bear's savage attention to Diane Nelson. But when Kyle Scholl was attacked, she knew the only way to quickly summon John Pex, who had the .30-06 and had fallen behind, was to yell continuously as a beacon to guide him in a straight line through the trees. John zeroed in, and with cool concentration diverted the bear from Diane with a stinging through-the-hump shot. Now the bear was five feet from the end of his rifle barrel.

No one would suspect a plant could have malevolence, not even a bush with as evil a name as "devil's club"—except, perhaps, the three people who nearly died because of where it grew.

These three, two men and a woman, were hiking down a watershed in rolling wooded foothills northwest of Alaska's Aleutian Range. They were headed for their helicopter rendezvous area in a meadow near eighty-mile-long Lake Iliamna, which is probably the world's largest red (or sockeye) salmon spawning grounds.

Kyle Scholl, twenty-three, and Diane Nelson, thirty-one, were walking almost abreast, but several feet apart, when they encountered a patch of thorny devil's club blocking their way. The shape of the bush suggested that the easiest path for Kyle was to the left. He took the suggestion. Diane stayed to the right.

John Pex, twenty-five, had fallen behind perhaps a hundred and fifty feet. He had traveled across some mossy vegetation covering the gaps between large boulders that appeared to be fairly solid footing. John broke through into a two-foot-deep hole, however, and wrenched and skinned his knee. He sat for a moment to rub it.

Although Diane and Kyle were now fifty feet apart, Diane kept up their conversation. Some of her sentences were more words than meaning, just because it was smart to make noise in bear country. This area, within thirty miles of Cook Inlet, is home to a considerable population of Alaska's coastal brown bears. It was July 24, 1985, and the red salmon were running. Obviously, attracting gigantic bears with one of the world's largest sockeye salmon spawning runs is one of the greatest reasons for caution. Noise prevents most sudden confrontations.

"I can see the meadow through the trees," Diane called. "Turn more to your right, Kyle, and you'll see it."

At that moment, Kyle parted the alders, stepped over a rise, and came face to face with a seven- to eight-hundred-pound sow flanked by a pair of three- to four-hundred-pound two-year-old cubs. The sow rose to her hind legs and gave a loud *woof* to spook her cubs to safety.

"Bear!" Kyle yelled back at Diane. "Bear! Bear!" Diane could see Kyle's orange pack flashing through the trees as he ran, trying to take advantage of the split-second head start the bear gave him by standing. Diane also saw the bear's huge head flash between the trees close behind Kyle.

He dove off to the side, hoping the bear would run past him. Instead, the agile sow lunged at his back. A big man, at six feet two inches, and almost two hundred pounds, Kyle was well known for his strength. While in school in Colorado, he had become a national champion wrestler. But he was helpless against the bear. All he could do was pull his knees under him, crouch under his backpack, and grip the mossy tundra with all of the strength he had. If she turned him over and got to his underside, he was finished.

The sow straddled Kyle, biting at the Cordura pack and the back of his head. The pack tore and released an eight-thousand-dollar surveying transit. She chomped it to pieces, breaking the laminated bolts that held it together, and then returned to Kyle. She clawed both sides of his shoulders, trying to turn him over, but Kyle held fast. She then bit at his head, ripping his scalp on the right side, and tore at the backpack so savagely that the padded strap left him with cuts and broad stripes of bruises. He raised his hand to protect his ear and head and she bit his thumb.

Bleeding profusely, Kyle felt himself weakening, about to release his hold. Bears seem to sense the moment when their prey gives up. They often sit back to watch for signs of life. And that is what this one now did. "Good," Kyle thought. "Maybe she'll quit now, if I don't move." But the sow pounced back and bit him twice on the right thigh.

"Oh God!"

This had been such a pleasant day, and the meadow was in view. If it weren't for the devil's club, he would have made that last two hundred yards at the end of the day without surprising an angry Alaska brown bear.

Working for the Bureau of Land Management, for four days Kyle and his colleagues had been cutting the boundary line for a particular 160-acre native land allotment. The surveyors' tent camp was set up next to the comparatively large airstrip at the small village of Iliamna, where sport anglers fly in and out to fish from lodges around the lake. Each morning, Vietnam veteran helicopter pilot Bob Campbell flew three crews of three people each to their respective survey sites. For Kyle, John, and Diane, it was a thirty-five-minute flight east to the vicinity of the even smaller village of Pedro Bay.

There was hardly a cloud in the sky that day. Flying low and hugging the shoreline, they could see vast schools of red salmon crowding into tributaries. Diane marveled at large fish trying to shove their way up tiny streams not more than a foot wide. John, who grew up hunting and fishing around Klamath Falls, Oregon, remembered twenty-five thousand salmon as being a good run up the Rogue River. Here he was seeing that many sockeyes in creeks that he could jump across. From the air, it appeared as if he could walk across their backs.

The land they were flown into to survey was on a beautifully green, rather steep, heavily wooded hillside. Unusual for Alaska, where hundred-year-old scrub spruce can measure only eight inches in diameter, some spruce on this slope measured thirty inches through. There was so much spruce, birch, or alder that it was impossible to survey a line without chainsawing the whole distance.

When the helicopter pilot returned to pick them up that evening, he couldn't see the crew through the dense trees. But he could easily see the cut-lines from the air and realized that they were finished on the west line and were cutting east on the north line. "Okay, I see you," Bob finally radioed. "But there's no flat area big enough for you to cut me out a place to land. I can see a meadow from up here. Just hike down that drainage you're working near, and it will take you out to a meadow. I'll be waiting there."

Caching their chain saws in the woods, Diane carried a radio and the transit's tripod, Kyle a radio and the transit, and John his rifle and a gas can. Soon after they began walking, Bob radioed again. "The meadow is marshy. My skids are sinking in the muck. I'll have to fly farther over to the sandy beach and wait there. Call me, and I'll pick you up when you reach the meadow."

The watershed was about fifty feet wide with an up-slope on either side. Diane was on the right slope when she saw the meadow through the alders. Kyle topped out on the left slope when he surprised the bear, although "surprised" is probably not an accurate description. Both Diane and Kyle had been deliberately making lots of noise. In addition, they felt confident that four days of constant chainsawing should have given the bears every opportunity to know their whereabouts and easily avoid confrontations.

Instead of a surprised bear, it was perhaps an angry bear. The cubs seemed too old for her to be that protective of them. And she made no threatening false or bluff charges as bears often do. She scattered her cubs and attacked viciously. Maybe the chainsawing humans had interrupted her fishing and kept her moving or hidden for four days. Perhaps she had all that she could take of both chain saws and helicopters by the time Kyle walked in on her hiding place.

Kyle was running toward Diane when the bear caught him. Diane dropped the tripod and ran toward John, yelling, "John! Bear! Bring the gun! A bear's got Kyle!"

John couldn't make out her words but assumed that she was yelling to chase off a bear. Running toward them, he fired two shots into the air to frighten the animal.

After sprinting about thirty feet, Diane stopped and looked back, desperate to help Kyle. She knew she couldn't fight a bear with a tripod, so she dropped it. Her only hope was to get John there with the gun—and she had better not delay things by leaving the vicinity and perhaps having to hunt for Kyle. She turned toward John, cupped her hands to her mouth, and because he could not see her through the trees, kept up a continuous yelling as a beacon for him to zero in on. It didn't occur to her to climb a tree. Yelling all the while, she lined up a certain tree and bush as a beeline route to Kyle. This was precisely the moment the bear had jumped on

Kyle and bit his thigh. And then, once again, the bear sat back to watch her victim.

Still yelling loudly and watching the bushes for John, Diane suddenly had the feeling of someone staring at the back of her neck. She turned to see why, and the bear's enormous head was so close that it filled her vision. Her horrible mouth was wide open, lunging for Diane's head. She doesn't remember the real pain, just the heavy thud when the bear hit. She felt a tooth hook under her eyebrow and another tooth puncture her skull above the left temple. Diane was on her knees, still not experiencing the real pain, but feeling the teeth on her skull and ripping at her scalp. All she could think of was squirming out of the bear's grip. It didn't work. She thought she could push herself away from the bear, but her arm was bitten for trying.

About the time Diane's yelling for John ceased, Kyle surmised that the bear had left him. Weak, but alive and determined to survive, he slowly turned his head for a look. No bear. But there was his radio! He reached out and switched it on. "Bob! I've been mauled by a bear!"

"Sure you have! When are you jokers getting out to the meadow?"

"GET THE MEDICS!" Kyle shouted into the radio.

Recognizing that Kyle was dead serious, Bob immediately lifted the helicopter off the ground for better radio transmission and called the Iliamna Airport. They, in turn, radioed Anchorage for a Lear jet, a doctor, and a nurse. Knowing that he wouldn't have enough fuel to complete the evacuation, Bob also asked for two Cessnas to meet them at Pedro Bay along with another helicopter to bring extra gasoline.

Immediately after John had fired the second shot, an obviously frightened cub galloped past so close that he could have touched it with the gun barrel. He thought at first that it was the bear that had been the cause of all of the yelling, but about two steps farther he saw the sow straddling Diane. The bear was shaking her by the head.

John's years as a hunter kept his nerves in check. No "buck fever." He was carrying his personal rifle, a Remington 760 pump-action .30-06. John had hunted elk and deer with this rifle, and handling it had become an automatic response.

The bear was broadside about fifty feet away. John had started with six cartridges in a ten-shot clip. Four were left. Afraid that he might hit Diane or that a bullet fragment might strike her, yet knowing that he must shoot immediately, John held high and risked one cartridge on a stinging, in-one-side-and-out-the-other shot in the sow's hump.

She immediately dropped Diane and charged John. In his helicopter, he had clocked bears running thirty-five to forty miles an hour through the brush, so he knew the angry animal would cover the fifty feet between them in seconds. By the time he pumped the second cartridge into the chamber and got the sights back on the sow, she was fifteen feet away and quartering slightly as she came around a tree that blocked her path. Aiming between her eyes, John pulled the trigger. The bullet hit her left eye and traveled under her scalp, but not into her brain.

Although it broke no bones, the impact of the bullet drove the bear's head down, almost between her front legs, slowing her for just an instant as John frantically chambered the third cartridge. The sow was within five feet, just off the end of the rifle barrel, and she lunged with her head high and her jaws open to attack when John fired. The bullet struck under the chin, blew the second vertebra out of the neck, and the huge bear fell. John instinctively chambered the next round. Although he can't remember doing it, John fired his last cartridge into her mouth, severing the tongue, and the sow rolled ten or fifteen feet and lodged against a tree.

John ran toward Diane, trying to reassure her by calling, "I think I got the bear!" Even in that desperate situation, Diane remembers his comment as amusing. "He thinks!" Actually, John wasn't wasting any time checking the bear. He had seen Diane being shaken by the head. He feared that her neck might be broken—no telling what else—and immediate first aid might be necessary to save her life. The sight of Diane's head didn't ease his fears.

Not knowing that Kyle had been attacked, too, John called, "Kyle! Come over here and help! Diane's been chewed by a bear!" Incredibly, Kyle got to his feet, and as John recalled later, "He came walking through the woods like nothing was wrong." John saw Kyle's torn scalp hanging down the back of his head and stopped him. Although Diane's wounds were more serious, Kyle was even more lacerated and bloody. John ran back and forth offering whatever first aid and comfort he could, while keeping a lookout for other bears. He was out of .30-06s but still had a shoulder-holstered .44 Magnum—not much of a weapon against brown bears.

After radioing for help, Bob flew across the lake, picked up Brent Jones and Kent Foster from another surveying crew, returned, and dropped them at the meadow. They wanted to build a stretcher to carry Kyle out, but he refused. The survival response that kept up his strength was anger. He swore at the bear. He pulled his sweatshirt hood over his head to hold his scalp in place; he didn't want anyone fooling with his wounds.

"I've gotta get out of here," he said. "The hell with the stretcher. I'm going now!"

Kyle stood, and Brent Jones stepped up to steady him. Kyle put an arm around Brent's neck, and they hobbled out the whole two hundred yards. About forty-five minutes later, by helicopter, and then by Cessna, he was at Iliamna.

Diane remembered the advice in her first-aid courses: to avoid further injury, possibly fatal, keep the victim quiet until qualified help arrives. Besides, she had tried to raise her head and felt consciousness slipping away. A self-reliant, self-sufficient person since childhood, Diane was terrified of blacking out and being unable to communicate her needs. She lay on her back, feeling her head. It seemed terribly disarranged and twice as big. Her left eye was severely damaged.

Diane became almost obsessive about getting her sweatshirt untied from her neck so that she could wrap her head and apply pressure. With her left arm nearly useless because of the bite, it was extremely difficult but she finally got her head wrapped. She could hear John talking with Bob on the radio but could see almost nothing. Blood from another cut one-quarter inch above her right brow was clouding her good eye.

John returned, still worried that Diane's neck might be broken. Using his shirt, he further wrapped her head and tried to splint her neck as best he could. When the other two surveyors hiked back from the helicopter, John added their shirts to her head bindings as well.

Knowing that Kyle had walked out, Diane raised herself on her elbows to see whether she could stand. Again, she felt about to lose consciousness.

"I can't," she said. "But I'm fine when I'm lying down. You'll have to make a stretcher."

The chain saws were far up the slope, but the men had Buck knives on their belts. The roots of young spruce don't reach far beyond the thick tundra, so the three men yanked two three-inch-thick saplings out of the ground. Limbs were whacked off. The roots were left on because they weren't in the way.

The three men buckled their belts and Diane's in loops around the two saplings. One surveyor had a raincoat in his pack and stretched it over the belts. Carefully, they carried her the two hundred yards to the meadow.

Diane was able to lie somewhat curled up on the backseat of the helicopter, so there was room for John to go along, too. The other two surveyors stayed behind, standing back to back with John's .44 Magnum, not knowing whether more bears were around, and fighting hordes of mosquitoes that covered their shirtless bodies. It was the longest twenty minutes of their lives until Bob could get Diane to Pedro Bay and return.

An emergency-medical-trained person was waiting for Diane with blankets to counter the chilling effects of shock. Able to stretch out on the seat of the Cessna, Diane was flown to Iliamna where Kyle was waiting in the Lear jet. Because of Bob Campbell's prompt and correct actions, Diane and Kyle received treatment in an Anchorage hospital within four hours of the attack.

Both patients required extensive layered stitching—Diane two thousand stitches and Kyle four thousand. Surgeons grafted skin from Kyle's leg and used tissue expanders (balloons under the skin) to stretch the skin so that the scalp could be gradually pulled back together. After four operations, the three-by-six-inch wound was reduced to a scar the width of a pencil.

Diane's decision to remain immobile proved critical. Her most dangerous wound was a skull puncture above the temple. Bone fragments could have floated off and lodged in her brain had she tried to walk. Her left eye was not blinded, but severed muscles and nerves prevent the lid from raising all of the way. The eyeball doesn't go up or down as far as it should, either, which causes double vision when the right eye moves farther than the left eye can follow.

"My middle field of vision is fine," she says happily. "I just move my head up or down to avoid double vision when I look in those directions, and carry on like normal. I can ski, drive a car, and everything!"

Two and a half years after the attack, Diane discovered that John's fear for her neck had been well founded. She had recurring headaches and tingling sensations down her arm. An MRI scan showed a damaged disk. Surgical removal of the disk and fusing the fifth and sixth vertebrae solved the problem.

Diane returned to work with the Bureau of Land Management, spending most of her time in the Anchorage office. She was back in the field in 1987 willing to return to field surveys as needed. Kyle spent the summer of 1986 surveying in central Alaska, then finished college, married, and moved to the Lower Forty-eight.

John Pex, whose skills as a hunter enabled him to save the lives of two friends, as well as his own, was awarded the Medal of Valor by then Secretary of the Interior, Donald Hodel, for his cool confrontation of the devil's club bear.

DINNER BELL BEARS

(As told by Jack Danielson)

Lloyd Oler ran when he thought Jack Danielson was dead, then stopped at a hundred yards to look back and see Jack dragging himself to his rifle. He was so elated to see Jack alive that he ran back to try getting him out of there, despite the fact that the sow and her two cubs were eating the deer just twenty yards away.

"Let's get out of here!" Lloyd shouted.

I didn't react as fast as my twenty-two-year-old partner. I was absorbed in boning out his deer, but I did look over my right shoulder to see what Lloyd was so excited about. My whole vision was filled with the enormous faces of three giant bears. They were side by side and running straight at me. I glanced at the rifles. They were five feet closer to the bears than they were to me. The rifles were even farther away from Lloyd, and there was no time.

I tried to rise from my kneeling position but didn't make it. The biggest bear, the one in the middle, bore down on me, head low like an attacking dog, and bit me in the right buttock. The impact threw me four feet. Lloyd hadn't moved much faster than me at first, but now he really moved. I remember seeing his running feet as I pitched forward.

I expected one of the other two bears to attack Lloyd. Biologists say that bears go for moving targets. Instead, the two other bears, obviously the sow's almost-adult cubs, grabbed the remains of the deer carcass and several bags of boned-out meat and then left.

I rolled when I hit the ground and came up with a hard kick to the bear's face with my left leg. As I fell back, three-inch eyeteeth clamped through my right leg. I felt one fang hit bone. I was yelling. The first bite hurt like hell. Also, I hoped that my yelling would chase off the bear. That didn't happen. I tried to jump up, thinking I'd get to my rifle. The bear slapped me down. One claw raked my forehead, another claw hooked my lip, and still another caught me under the chin.

When I tried to get to my knees, the sow slapped me back and forth with a sweeping cuff across the back and then another to my left shoulder. She was standing over me, mouth open, probably growling. I can't remember any of the sounds. I grabbed her by the muzzle, trying to fend off another bite. I couldn't. Again, she bit my left leg. My brain was no longer registering the excruciating pain that I had felt with the first bite, but I was fighting for my life. I pulled hair out of the bear's face and even tried to gouge her eyes, but she didn't seem to feel the paltry pain that I was able to inflict. At that point, I knew that I'd never get to the rifles.

The bear released my leg, and I lay there, feeling helpless. She was too big, too quick, and too skilled in using her claws and teeth. She seemed to anticipate my every move, and at forty-nine, my moves weren't fast.

I couldn't believe that it was happening to me. I had hunted deer on Alaska's Afognak Island twice before. I had seen one bear during the first hunt and a lot of bear signs during the second, but we'd had absolutely no trouble with bears.

Four of us had intended to hunt, but two men dropped out, so Lloyd and I went by ourselves. I hadn't known Lloyd Oler for very long, but he grew up deer hunting in Wisconsin, so I figured that we'd do just fine. We were flown in on Sunday, November 2, 1986, and the pilot was scheduled to pick us up the next Saturday. At my suggestion, we set up camp about two hundred yards from the place where the camp had been before. The new campsite was on a little bluff above the beach and a safe distance from the river, where we knew bears would come to catch salmon.

We hung a few cans and metal cups on a cord that circled the camp to give us a few seconds of warning if a bear came prowling into camp. We did sleep with guns beside us, just in case. I had brought a 12-gauge shotgun and buckshot loads for that purpose. Lloyd had his .308 Heckler & Koch semiautomatic rifle. We ate dried food that had no meat smells to attract bears. Afognak is 250 miles southeast of Anchorage and just forty-five minutes by air from Kodiak Island. The same strain of enormous brown bear lives on both islands, so these precautions seemed sensible. Beyond that, however, our only concern about the big bears was that Lloyd wanted to see one.

With an estimated ten thousand deer on the island and a week to hunt, there was no rush to make a kill. Lloyd and I hunted together so that he could learn his way around before taking off on his own. I took him up through the mushy tundra lowland to about twelve to fifteen hundred feet. It's pretty country on the two-thousand-foot mountains where most of the deer live. That's where the bears hunt deer, too, but as I said, there had been no trouble before.

On the second day, we saw a bear's den dug into a south-facing slope. Fresh dirt was scattered below the hole, but Lloyd didn't see his bear. No one seemed to be at home.

By Wednesday, Lloyd figured that he knew his way around, and about a thousand feet up the slope, we separated. He wanted to take a stand, and I meandered through the jack pines, hoping to kick something out, either for myself or to move the deer toward Lloyd. I was a mile away when I heard one shot from his .308. At the time, I had no clue that what I heard was a dinner bell.

I wanted to get to Lloyd fast, so I walked up a dry streambed to a rock outcropping where I could look down and possibly locate my partner. I searched with binoculars and saw him about two hundred yards away. He was field dressing a nine-point buck. He had dragged the 160-pound animal twenty yards from the edge of the woods where the deer had fallen. Going farther into the open might have been safer, but twenty yards of uphill drag no doubt had been difficult enough.

I touched off a round with my .300 Winchester Magnum to let him know that I was on my way to help. I didn't realize that I had rung the dinner bell again.

"Nice deer, Lloyd," I said when I got to him.

"Dropped him right over there," Lloyd said, nodding toward the edge of the spruces and firs. He picked up his rifle to pose for a picture, and I took several.

I started boning out the venison and cutting two-foot sections of sock-like game-bag material in which to carry the meat. Lloyd tied the mouths of the socks.

I was cutting the last of the tenderloin off the backbone when Lloyd heard a twig snap, looked up to see what had caused it, and yelled, "Let's get out of here!" As I said earlier, the biggest bear, a sow that I believe weighed about nine hundred pounds, bit, clawed, and hit me until I was on the ground and almost ready to give up. Her cubs, two-year-olds, carried our meat and most of what was left of the deer into the trees.

I couldn't tell where the sow was because I was lying on the ground. I couldn't see at all with my left eye. It was either gone or filled with blood. I was afraid to move and afraid to stay where I was. I decided to take the chance and run.

The bear was just to my rear and jumped on me like a cat. She rolled me with another cuff, and I came back up on my feet. She rose with me, always anticipating my moves. I don't know whether or not I made it all the way up, but I do remember looking right at her breasts. She swatted me again, this time tearing off two old sweaters with one swipe and leaving me with only one sleeve. I fell to my knees. Again, she sank her teeth into my right thigh and buttock. I felt the buttock tear when she lifted me off the ground. I hung there helpless, and then she dropped me.

The bear glanced up at Lloyd as though to see whether anyone else cared to fight her for the deer. He had gotten maybe a hundred yards away and maybe five yards into the trees. You don't get very far very fast in high underbrush. Lloyd was horrified, and he was certain that I was dead. When the bear looked up at him, he figured that it was his turn. But he didn't move, so the sow picked up a chunk of deer that the cubs had left behind and joined them.

I lay there, worrying about broken bones and bleeding to death. There were too many holes. All of the bites were concentrated in the right leg, so I tried to lift it. It moved, so there were no broken bones or cut tendons.

The afternoon sky was gray-blue, and the sow was gray-brown. She blended well with the trees and shadows, but with my right eye, I could see that she had taken the dominant position by lying over the remains of the deer. All three bears were popping bones and chomping noisily. I dragged myself across the ground to my rifle, rolled over to position my legs toward the bear, and rested the barrel in the V of my crossed feet. If the sow moved toward me again, she'd pay with her life.

Lloyd was so excited when he saw that I was alive that he ran down to join me, despite the fact that the bears were only twenty yards away and eyeing him.

"Jack," he whispered, trying to help me to my feet, "we've got to get you out of here. Can you walk?"

"I think I'm bleeding to death," I told him, almost under my breath.

Lloyd checked my wounds and opened the boot that I thought was filling with blood. "Lots of lymph fluid," he whispered. "Only a little blood coming out of the thigh wounds."

"How bad are they?"

"I can see the bone and an artery pulsing, but it's not bleeding."

"I'm going into shock."

"No, you're not!" Lloyd told me, forcing himself to whisper. "You're going to make it. Let's get you on your feet."

I was shaky. It was an effort to stand. But Lloyd wiped the clotted blood from my left eye with a piece of game bag, and I could see out of it. I saw the sow watching us. A tightly wrapped piece of game bag slowed the bleeding over my eye. Lloyd picked up his camera, rifle, and a ten-pound sack of meat that the bears had missed. There was no time to look for my glasses. My knife had been knocked out of my hand, too. Lloyd helped me get my backpack on. I grabbed my rifle, and we started.

Lloyd helped me through the brush and out of the bears' sights. But I was afraid that it was only a matter of time until the bears devoured the deer and would look for more. Maybe Lloyd shouldn't have taken that sack of meat, but it really made little difference. The scent of blood—the deer's and mine—was all over us.

It was slow going. My wounds were numb, so I didn't feel much pain, but it was hard to stay on my feet. We were walking sideways, rifles pointed back toward the bears.

"Lloyd, no guns off safety," I said. "We could shoot ourselves getting away." Sure enough, he had slipped his safety off to be ready for the bear, but he put it back on.

"I've got to stop, Lloyd," I said a few minutes later. "There's no feeling in my side. I'm going into shock."

"You're not! Keep walking!" he told me.

Something was moving in the woods. It sounded like the bears. Lloyd's rifle went to his shoulder, but the bears didn't come into view.

"Lloyd, you've got to guide me right to camp on the first try," I told him.

"I will," he assured me.

"If we miss, I won't have the strength for another try."

"Don't worry, I'll do it."

I really didn't believe that he could. He hadn't yet spent enough time on Afognak.

Again, something was running in the woods. Lloyd's rifle snapped to his shoulder. But whatever it was didn't show itself.

The numbness was leaving. Lloyd let me sit long enough so that I could make sure that the bleeding hadn't started again.

"Jack, you're not bleeding to death, and you're not going into shock." He kept trying to talk me out of going into shock. Apparently, it was working.

I heard water running just ahead. I staggered into the stream. "Lloyd, maybe the water will eliminate some of our blood scent. It'll be easier to walk, too." We walked in the stream for a while.

Finally, he said that we'd have to leave the stream. He led me through the muskeg and willows. Incredibly, an hour and a half after the attack, Lloyd led me right into camp. It was just getting dark.

Carelessly, we had brought no disinfectant, no medicine, and no bandages. Of course, we had no radio to call for help, either. It was Wednesday, and the pilot wouldn't be back until Saturday. Lloyd got water and boiled it to clean me up. At least we had dish soap and salt, and Lloyd dissolved some in water. He sponged the warm mixture into the punctures. Some holes were the size of quarters; a couple were like half-dollars. Another two, low on my buttock, were torn punctures. You could see daylight through my leg where two canine teeth had met.

Lloyd kept worrying about lockjaw. I didn't know whether the tetanus booster I'd had a few years earlier would kill off bacteria from a bear's mouth, but losing the leg worried me more. We kept the Coleman lantern burning all night. My shotgun pointed to the back of the tent, Lloyd's assault rifle to the front.

I was in and out of consciousness all night. I slept fitfully and drank huge amounts of water.

Lloyd was optimistic on Thursday morning. We had a blaze orange survival blanket to stake out as a signal, and we had 12-gauge flares for my shotgun. There is considerable boating activity around Afognak, mostly fishing boats, and planes are always bringing hunters in or taking them out.

Lloyd was right! Around noon, a two-engine plane began circling. He ran out onto the bluff and waved his blaze orange hat. The plane flew on. The crews aboard the boats offshore didn't notice the flares we fired.

At about 2:00 P.M., Lloyd was again elated. A floatplane had landed in the bay. Certain that the pilot had responded to our blaze orange blanket, Lloyd ran to the water's edge, waving and yelling frantically to get his attention. There was no way to get out to the plane, of course, and twenty minutes later, it took off. The pilot never heard Lloyd.

"Back to square one," Lloyd thought in despair, when suddenly four hunters appeared on the other side of the river. The plane had dropped them off, and they had heard Lloyd's cries. He explained our plight, and at low tide, the men, all members of a Mormon church in Homer, came across to help. They pulled my head wound together with one-hundred-mile-an-hour aircraft tape, cleaned wounds and tried to push first-aid cream into the punctures. Unfortunately, at thirty-five to forty degrees, the cream came out of the tube as thick as toothpaste and wouldn't stay in the wounds. One of the men placed a ten-foot cross made of aluminum foil on the beach as a distress signal.

The Mormons also fired a number of three-shot distress signals with their deer rifles when they thought that boats were within hearing. Even then, none of us realized that they were ringing the dinner bell again.

That night was bad. Lloyd remembered some mothballs that his wife had sent along in his gear and scattered them around camp in the hope that the strong odor would repel bears. I was too miserable to worry about bears. Loss of blood and body fluids and the resultant dehydration were taking their toll.

I was hurting bad and thought that I'd never leave the tent alive.

At about 9:00 P.M., a bear—perhaps attracted by the dinner bell—gave a *woof* in the woods. We believed that it smelled a mothball. I woke Lloyd, but it made no attempt to enter our tent.

At 2:30 A.M., I heard a bear again, and we found out that the Mormons had heard two bears growl at each other right in their camp. The hunters ran out of their tents firing pistol shots and sloshed gasoline on the smoldering campfire. They stood guard back to back for the rest of the night.

By Friday morning, I was sore all over. The sky was overcast and a storm was brewing. I knew from experience that when that kind of weather develops, the planes don't fly.

Suddenly, Lloyd was shouting that a floatplane had landed. Steve Larsen, our Island Air Service bush pilot, had seen the cross on the beach. Quickly, I was loaded aboard the plane. The tide was going out, and Larsen was worried about not being able to take off because the water was becoming too shallow for the plane's pontoons. I was rushed to the hospital on Kodiak Island.

Recovery took months because of the many different bacteria from the bear's mouth. More than a year later, the torn buttock hasn't quite returned to normal, and I walk with a slight limp, but plans are being made to hunt Afognak Island deer in the future. The next time, however, one of us will stand guard with a heavy rifle while the other guts out and bones the meat. I am convinced, as are many others, that at least some of the brown bears on the island have learned to regard rifle shots as dinner bells—chances to easily acquire meat or at least a gut pile. I don't blame the bears, and I hold no grudge against the one that attacked me. The island is theirs, and we take our chances when we invade it. But I'll be better prepared next time.

The Bear's Dinner Bell

Apparently, some brown bears are attracted by "dinner bell" rifle shots, according to Sterling Miller, bear biologist for the Alaska Department of Fish and Game. Other hunters besides Jack Danielson have reported similar incidents. Roger Smith, who managed the Afognak and Kodiak bear population under Miller, believes that the decades of big-game hunting on the islands have conditioned some bears to associate shooting with food. Studies are underway.

Lee Garlock, one of the four Mormons who helped Danielson, said that the bad weather that developed just after Jack was flown from the island caused several groups of Afognak hunters to assemble while waiting for transportation. Bear problems were a hot topic of conversation. One party of hunters lost a hanging deer carcass to a bear at night, which could have happened regardless of the dinner bell response. A third group, however, had the meat of one deer on a backboard. When they shot a second deer, a brown bear charged in, ripped the meat from the backboard and proceeded to eat it right there. The hunters fired over the bear's head in an effort to chase it off. Unafraid of rifle shots, the bear continued to eat, and the men promptly left.

Bears are highly intelligent animals, and cubs stay with the sows long enough to learn much from their mothers. The two-year-olds accompanying the sow that attacked Jack Danielson, if the theory is correct, had already learned that rifle shots may mean meat or at least a gut pile. In this way, a certain form of behavior can be gradually spread through an entire bear population. Remember that most hunters on Afognak are hunting deer and do not have bear tags. They are therefore very reluctant to shoot a meat-raiding bear unless they are forced to do so by a dangerous attack.

Dr. Clyde Deal, the Kodiak physician who treated Jack Danielson, forcefully recommended that every wilderness hunter have a complete first-aid kit including disinfectants and a broad-spectrum antibiotic.

Dr. Louis Mayer, an Anchorage physician who is also a big-game guide with nineteen years experience, made the same point and went on to discuss safety considerations. He recommended that hunters make themselves aware of dangerous quirks in local bear behavior by checking with guides and Department of Fish and Game personnel who work in the hunting area. He also said that when one hunter dresses out a deer, a partner should always stand guard with a heavy rifle. Do the gutting out and any other work as far out into an open area as possible because big bears are extremely fast on their feet.

Looking back on his experience, Jack Danielson believes that the bear wasn't trying to kill him but was only trying to get rid of him in the same way that a sow gets rid of an aggressive boar when she is not in estrus. Unfortunately, he says that he fought back without thinking. He struggled, and that may have prolonged the attack. If he had not resisted, Danielson thinks, the bear may have ceased the attack after the first bite.

TUNDRA TERROR

The polar bear jumped gorilla fashion on the man's chest, jumping up and down as if he were killing a seal.

November 24, 1993. "You fellows, stay alert." The security guard's words hung as a coda to the grim report that had just been delivered to the tiny population of Oliktok Point radar site: two polar bears were definitely roaming nearby, and a third had been seen in the vicinity earlier. It seemed the bears were drawn to the tiny outpost near the Beaufort Sea in northernmost Alaska by butchered bowhead whale meat that Inupiat Indians had stored near their fishing cabins, a mere three hundred yards away. Under ideal conditions, polar bears are able to smell food from twenty miles. With the bears already in the neighborhood, it was only a matter of time before they investigated cooking and garbage odors coming from the radar site as well.

Oliktok Point once housed dozens of military personnel as a link in the "DEW line," the United States' highly secret Distant Early Warning defense network guarding against over-the-pole attack from the Soviet Union. But with the thawing of the Cold War, the site crew was gradually pared down to a civilian staff of six, and security patrols had been eliminated.

Which is why sympathetic ARCO security guards from the nearby Kuparuk oil field frequently shared what they knew with Oliktok personnel.

Alex Polakoff, fifty-three, a hunter and thirteen-year veteran of the DEW line sites, but a recent arrival at Oliktok, took bears very seriously.

He had heard the horror stories. In 1985, a polar bear stuck its head through the kitchen window and had to be beaten back with a pool cue and an iron skillet. Another time, a driver delivering water from Prudhoe Bay was chased up a twenty-foot fuel tank ladder by a bear that surprised him from behind his truck. A site worker ran it off with a bulldozer. The next bear in camp was a grizzly. Back in 1990, near Point Lay radar site over on the Arctic Ocean, an Inupiat couple were confronted by an emaciated polar bear as they walked down a dark street. To secure his pregnant girlfriend's escape, the courageous twenty-eight-year-old man faced down the bear with his pocketknife. Fifty pounds of his body were eaten.

Alex's fellow Oliktok crewmember, mechanic Don Chaffin, fifty-five, was less concerned, almost cavalier, about polar bears. On one occasion Alex complained that the site's Chevy Suburban ought to be plugged into the living quarters building to keep the engine from freezing, arguing that he shouldn't have to risk a two-hundred-yard walk in the dark to the garage every time he was required to go to the airstrip in the middle of the night. Don chided him. "Alex is afraid the polar bears will get him." True. He was. Alex had also been frustrated by what he considered the lack of concern exhibited by both the Air Force, which owned the site, and Martin Marietta Services, which had contracted to run it.

Oliktok was built in the 1950s by sledding twenty-by-twenty-foot insulated aluminum modules into place, raising them onto pilings, and joining them end to end. The site was composed of a "train" of these modules three hundred feet long in which the six men lived and worked. Despite the fact that a leaping polar bear can reach as high as sixteen feet, the windowsills were built only five feet off the floor. The six-foot pilings would raise the total height of the windows to ten or eleven feet above ground level. This safety cushion was somewhat compromised, however, by road gravel and snowdrifts that had accumulated alongside the building. Recent tracks under and along the building indicated that a bear had been looking in the outpost windows—windows that were snap-in, double-pane, and without security bars.

But what clinched the employees' status as bear bait in Alex's mind was the firearms rule. Each man could have a rifle, a shotgun, and a pistol for hunting and hiking, but they were kept in a locked gun safe and signed out as needed. The gun safe was mounted six inches off the floor between some lockers, its lock mounted so low it could be reached only by kneeling.

On November 26, a Nuiqsut villager killed one of the three bears that had been reported by the ARCO guard, and the sense of vigilance intensified around the compound. Within the next few days, biologist Richard Shideler was even invited to Oliktok to suggest means to better bear-proof the site. His recommendations: Increased outdoor lighting; doors that opened outward and closed against strong inside metal frames; bars over the windows; the removal of road material close to buildings; an end to storing garbage cans on the porch; chain-link skirting to prevent bears from hiding under buildings; perhaps even substantial iron cages surrounding outside doors so personnel could appraise the situation in safety before leaving. According to Shideler, no immediate actions were taken.

At 8:30 P.M. on the night of November 30, just hours after Shideler left, Don and support services worker Gary Signs, thirty-eight, were sitting on stools at the bar in the dayroom. Don was hunched over a crossword puzzle, his back to the window. On the bar's opposite side, Gary was working on a report when his peripheral vision caught a movement at the window. Polar bear!

Don looked up, saw Gary staring past him, and swiveled toward the window.

Gary says Don slapped his magazine at the window to frighten off the bear, but Don recalls no such action. "Let's get out of here!" Gary yelled as he raced to the fire door leading to an adjacent room. The bear's head dropped below the three-foot-wide window frame as Don stumbled over a stool, trying to escape from behind the bar. Gary pulled the magnetic latch, stepped inside the doorway, and held the door for Don. After regaining his balance, Don sidestepped the stool and was rounding the bar when he heard glass explode. He looked back and yelled, "Oh, no!"

Like smashing ice to get at a seal, the polar bear leaped through the shattered window in a shower of glass, taking the frame with it. The giant animal landed beside Don and reared up in his terrified face. Don, still several feet from Gary in the doorway, grabbed the bear's muzzle in an attempt to protect himself. But the bear, standing a full foot taller than his six feet, stretched its head and neck forward and sunk its teeth into his jaw. With almost superhuman effort, he pushed against the bear's black nose and tore himself free for an instant, only to have his hand and arm severely bitten. As if experimenting with how best to kill its unusual prey, the bear began swatting its victim.

A terrible realization came to Gary as he watched this bloody encounter. The gun safe was in the next room, but the key was in an office two hundred feet in the opposite direction! He would have to scramble around the bear to get to it, and even if he made it, there was a good chance Don would be dead by the time he got back. Should he close the door and sacrifice Don to save himself and the other four?

The bear solved this dilemma by batting Don's 240-pound body through the doorway. Gary bolted for the opposite door, found a phone, dialed the public address system, and screamed, "Bear in building!" With nothing else at hand, he grabbed a fire extinguisher and rushed back. The bear was on top of Don now, biting at the back of his head.

Don could feel fangs grating on his skull. He saw flashes of lightning and felt a neck vertebra snap. He thought blood filling his right eye was blinding him, but, in fact, his eyeball was now resting on his cheek. He could only weakly cry, "Help me."

Gary aimed the extinguisher's nozzle at the polar bear. A weak stream of water arced into its face. It raised its head and looked quizzically at Gary, and then merely resumed its grim work on Don.

Mechanic Joe Peterson, thirty-seven, hadn't been able to make out the loud message over the public address system, but he heard a commotion and came running to investigate. Grabbing the extinguisher from Gary, he shouted, "Go get the gun case key!" Not a chance, thought Gary. The bear was now ten feet from the gun safe. Even if he already had the key, it would be sure suicide to kneel that close to the bear while fiddling with the lock. Right now, he had to find something more persuasive than a dribbling fire extinguisher. He ran to the hallway and grabbed another extinguisher, this time a Halon model that would suck oxygen from the air and produce a distracting—he hoped—*whoosh*.

He came back into the gun safe room just in time to see Joe throw the empty extinguisher at the bear. Gary handed the second extinguisher to him and was running for a third when Alex arrived on the scene and was able to make out white fur through the thick haze of Halon fog.

Alex's hair stood on end and his strong fear of bears put him in a primal "fight or flight" mode. He raced back to his room and grabbed his fully loaded Mossberg 500. He had brought the gun from his previous work site, intending to store it in the gun safe, but had hid the gun in his room when he saw the unsafe conditions at Oliktok.

When he returned, he saw the bear jumping up and down on Don. He approached to within seven feet, squatted so that the slug's upward trajectory would be safely away from his unfortunate co-worker, and fired into the bear's broad chest.

No visible reaction.

He fired a second slug into the animal's chest. The bear rose from Don in slow motion and walked through a door into a small library room. Alex stepped to his left and fired two more slugs that he hoped would find the bear's chest. Of the four ounce-and-a-half slugs from the three-inch 12-gauge Magnum, one found the polar bear's heart. The animal dropped dead.

Gary and Joe got the key, retrieved their rifles, and hurried out to search for the third bear that had been sighted. Alex was left behind to make Don comfortable and try to keep him talking so that he wouldn't go into shock. "I'm cold," the badly mauled man mumbled, choking on his blood. Alex covered him with a blanket, slid a pillow under his head, and jammed an upholstered chair into the shattered window in an attempt to block the wind current carrying minus twenty- to thirty-degree temperatures. He had already called the ARCO oil site for an ambulance.

In the confusion, the paramedics thought the message was for them to pick up a corpse. They were leisurely driving down the road when Alex frantically waved them to the living quarters. A police officer from Prudhoe Bay, fifty miles away, arrived at 3:00 A.M. to check out "the shooting" and wanted to confiscate the shotgun. "The bear is lying over there—take a look," Alex said. "If you take my gun, take me, too. I'm not staying in this place without it."

Emergency room personnel at Providence Hospital in Anchorage, where Don was being flown, told Betty Chaffin that her husband had been shot in the back of the head and would be dead on arrival. That same misinformation—probably influenced by a missing patch of scalp at the back of Don's head—even had Alex worried when he heard it. Was it possible that a slug hit bone and deflected downward, killing his friend? It was 6:00 A.M. before a nurse called to say that Don was alive and, in fact, not shot.

Eventually, Don was left with a numb left leg, a numb right hand that drops things, five hundred stitches, and a hundred fifty staples in the back of his head, seven metal plates in his head, forty inches of scars in his head and face, and double vision (after several operations to his damaged right eye, it still tracks five degrees lower than the left). Although his medical bills are paid by workman's compensation, he claims he has lost all ability to earn a living.

A week after the attack, Richard Shideler found portable lights on loan from ARCO still at the radar site, but no recommended structural changes were initiated. He heard nothing further from either Martin Marietta or the Air Force. At some point, however, one-inch plywood was nailed over the windows.

On December 2, 1993, USAF and Martin Marietta personnel visited the site and immediately relaxed the firearms rules: one firearm would be available in each wing. Gary Signs and Joe Peterson were given plaques and commended for bravery. In a printed reprimand from Martin Marietta, R. E. Cunningham, the manager of communications, electronics, and meteorology acknowledged that had it not been for Alex's quick response, a far greater tragedy might have occurred. The balance of the letter, however, makes it clear that saving Don Chaffin's life, and perhaps his own and others' as well, was no excuse for violating project policy and procedures.

Three days after the attack, Alex Polakoff left and never again worked at Oliktok Point. He made Utah his home, but misses Alaska's vast wilderness.

THE GRIZZLY JINX

Three miles an hour is brisk walking, but severely mauled Ralph Borders and his brother-in-law, Bill Gonce, made the five miles back to the spike camp in one hour. The packer, verging on panic, boosted Ralph into his saddle, then ran two miles ahead of the horse to the cabins, screaming, "Bear attack!" as they came down the slope. Leroy Sewell ran out, took one look, and sprinted four and a half miles in ankle- to knee-deep snow to a three-wheeler to finish the balance of nine miles to the nearest radio-telephone.

Bill Gonce pointed to the tracks in the snow. "Wolf," said his brother-in-law, Ralph Borders.

Both men turned downslope to watch for the animal. Clearly, the tracks were only minutes old. Snow had been falling for almost an hour. Seeing nothing on the open mountainside, the men resumed climbing upward toward one final vantage point to glass for Dall sheep before the day ended. Within yards, they found cause for the wolf's departure. Paralleling the canine prints were equally fresh bear tracks.

As Bill turned his head to see the rows of tracks, he caught movement from the corner of his eye. "There they are."

"Where?" Ralph asked, thinking Bill had spotted sheep.

"Right there." Ralph turned and saw the terrifying sight—three grizzlies less than fifty feet above them. It seemed incredible that the bears could have remained hidden as the men approached. The brush at that elevation was less than a foot high. The grizzlies had been lying behind the lip of a depression with the sow facing away from the two men, but now, she was looking over her shoulder. Her two cubs were behind her on their feet. As soon as the sow made eye contact with the men, she turned and charged downhill, seemingly all in one motion.

Borders had spent considerable time hunting and filming Alaskan bears, and he instantly recognized the cubs as in their third year—nearly mature and only about a hundred pounds lighter than their five-hundred-pound mother. He had experienced two charges before by sows with cubs. Both times had been bluffs, and he had scared off the bears by firing his .458 revolver (now at home) into the ground near them and slightly to the side to avoid a ricochet hit. Now Ralph desperately tried to chamber a cartridge in his .338. The rifle had always needed help accepting that first round.

Oddly, even as the sow charged, she didn't appear angry to Ralph. No red-eyed rage, bared teeth, or growling threats to suggest she was defending her cubs. But he knew this sow was too close to be bluffing. Perhaps she mistook the men for caribou or other prey that she could have easily run down at this distance.

The younger bears charged as well. One cub's head was even with its mother's right hip. The second cub was about the same distance behind the first. As the sow closed in, she glanced back and forth between the men twice, making her choice. Ralph was a yard or so nearer. She locked her eyes on him as he frantically attempted to work the bolt closed.

Bill had carried his .30-06 fully loaded. He slipped off the safety, but hesitated. Which grizzly should he shoot? He had never hunted bears, and all three looked fully grown to him. Before he could shoulder his rifle, the sow seized Ralph's arm at the biceps and carried him past Gonce without breaking stride. That left Bill's rifle pointing somewhere beneath the chin of the first cub—just five feet away. Thinking it was already too late, he pulled the trigger.

This hunt had been jinxed from day one. High winds had prevented pilot Bill Sewell from landing near the upper cabin (located at an elevation of four thousand feet) that the brothers-in-law had expected to use. Instead, they had been forced to fly into a camp a packer was using at twenty-five hundred feet—more than fifteen miles from where they planned to hunt. That was Sunday evening. Sewell promised to return Tuesday, weather permitting, and fly them the rest of the way. Meanwhile, they could hunt the peaks near this camp, located about sixty miles southeast of Fairbanks. The packer's sidewall tent had no stove, but at least it was shelter.

On Monday, they carried sleeping bags and a two-man tent and set up a spike camp at the end of the day's hunt. By Tuesday afternoon, they had counted a wolf, about a hundred caribou, and three Dall ewes—but no rams. Another front was blowing in, so they returned to the packer's camp knowing Sewell would not be able to make good his promise. Snow fell all day Wednesday, confining them to camp.

Bill and Ralph, both Alaska residents, understood fickle weather. By Thursday, realizing that they couldn't be flown to the cabin they had originally planned to use, the two hunters decided to hike nine miles up Dry Creek to another set of cabins they knew of. They would later set up another spike camp three miles beyond.

Luck continued to elude them. After hunting their way up to the camp, they found three sheep hunters already in residence at the better of the two cabins. They stayed in an older cabin to the rear. The wood stove didn't work, so they made dinner of some chocolate and crawled into their sleeping bags.

Friday morning, they hiked the remaining two miles to their designated spike campsite. Twenty ewes and lambs were in plain view on a mountainside across Dry Creek Valley. The best chances of finding rams would be three more miles up the north side of the valley. By lunchtime, they were ready to climb a ridge sloping up to a sixty-five-hundred-foot mountain. Ralph would later remember that as they ate they saw tracks of a sow bear with cubs, but they didn't appear fresh.

Two hours later, the hunters slipped over a saddle at fifty-five hundred feet and spent an hour glassing a huge bowl. Bill glanced at his watch—4:00 P.M. No sheep. And nothing was set up at camp. But he had noticed a ledge a hundred yards higher from which another large bowl could be glassed. "While we're this close," he said to his partner, "why not make sure we didn't miss any sheep. The climb will warm us. Then we'd better get back."

Ralph agreed. Halfway to the ledge they saw the tracks that, behind a shallow depression, led to the mother of all jinxes: three charging grizzlies.

Bill's shot so surprised and stung the lead cub that, even at five feet, it spun around and tried to leap, but instead, rolled onto its sibling. Both cubs took the warning and disappeared up the mountain in a clatter of rocks.

The sow carried Ralph thirty feet past Bill, and then lost her balance on the steep incline. As she fell, she wrapped her forelegs loosely around Ralph, and together they rolled fifty feet down the slope, the rifle skittering out of reach. Ralph remembers thinking that the sow must have fed on the blueberries and low bush cranberries that he had walked through on the way up. Her breath didn't stink.

At the end of the long tumble, the bear loosed her grip on him and came to a halt downhill. He was on his back. He tried to flip over to protect his stomach, but the bear grabbed his right arm. For the second time he thought, "That's okay. Chewing an arm can't do killing damage."

The sow dropped his arm and suddenly slashed her teeth into his face—not chewing, but ripping as she rose up on her hind legs, front paws high, to lunge and rip again. Bill, who could only hope that his friend was still alive, turned away from the fleeing cubs just as Ralph yelled, "Bill, get her off me!"

Bill was afraid he might hit his friend, but what choice did he have? His variable scope was on low power, so at fifty feet, his field of vision included both Ralph and the bear. Just as the sow rose again from another slashing attack—the fourth, Ralph would later remember—Bill centered the crosshairs on her shoulder. The bear reacted to the shot by instantly biting into Ralph's left leg. Again, she reared up. Bill's second shot knocked her clear of Ralph, but only for an instant.

Bill closed the bolt on the last cartridge in his rifle. The bear pounced down on Ralph's right ankle and reared up, still gripping it as Bill fired.

Ralph felt a stabbing pain in his ankle and thought he was shot. But the sow had bitten down when the bullet struck her spine. She collapsed across his legs.

He pulled out from under the bear. His first concern was that he would not be able to walk with a shot ankle. They were five miles from the spike camp, seven from the cabins, and it was already 4:00 P.M. "Help me find my glasses," he yelled, "We gotta go!"

Bill's priority, however, was reloading in case the cubs returned. Ralph began crawling up the trail he had rolled down. He found his hat and pulled it over his head to hold together ripped flesh and help stanch the bleeding. He had felt teeth scrape his skull on the first attack. At least his ankle hadn't been shot—he could walk. And for the moment, he wasn't feeling pain. But he knew he soon would. There was no time to waste: by 7:30 it would be dark.

Halfway up the slope, Ralph found his glasses. At the spot where the incident began, an eighteen-inch patch of blood indicated that the cub had been hit and probably wouldn't return.

The descent from the fifty-five-hundred-foot elevation went quickly, despite Ralph's wounds. Once again, Bill wanted to check the injuries. This childhood friend from Anaheim, California, was missing two-thirds of his upper lip and couldn't close his mouth. This buddy for whom he had arranged a job in Haines, Alaska, was wiping blood from his glasses with his fingers. This man who had married his sister Ellen, now had wounds on his head, both arms, right leg, and left foot. There was no telling how much more damage was beneath his torn and bloody clothes.

An hour after the attack, they had traveled the five miles back to their spike camp. The packer was there when they arrived. Verging on panic, the packer boosted Ralph into a saddle, and then ran ahead, leading his horse. Bill, still carrying the daypack, ran behind the horse for two miles to the sheep hunters' cabins.

"Bear attack!" the packer screamed as they barreled down the slope to the cabins. Leroy Sewell, brother of the pilot, ran out. He took one look at Ralph and figured the man would bleed to death if not medivaced out quickly. Strapping on his 8-mm Mauser, he headed out—he had to reach a gold-mining cabin nine miles away that had a radio-telephone. Sewell ran four and a half miles in ankle- and knee-deep snow to where a three-wheeler was cached. Then he sped to the cabin where miner Pat Peede called 911.

The available helicopters were on maneuvers at Fort Greely, but one was dispatched immediately—it didn't even take time to refuel. The pilot scanned Dry Creek Valley for cabins with mules outside but couldn't find any. He turned back. On the ground Peede redialed 911. "Can you patch me in with the chopper?" he asked. "They're heading in the wrong direction."

The emergency operator could only relay messages, so Peede and Sewell arranged to stand on a hillside with a lantern so the helicopter could spot them. The pilot landed for specific directions, and then flew on to pick up Ralph.

Fearing Ralph might not make it through the night, Bill pleaded to go along to the hospital with his friend. The pilot eventually agreed and strapped Bill to the ceiling of the helicopter in a stretcher. He was given earphones and could hear the pilot talking to his base.

"The twenty-minute light is on," the pilot said, worried about fuel. But twenty minutes later, they still hadn't landed. "The light is out," the pilot said. "We're an accident waiting to happen."

The tower at Fort Greely tried to direct them around a snow squall as they neared the base. There wasn't enough fuel for that. "Then go over it at twenty-five hundred feet," the controllers directed them. The pilot refused. "We're on empty. Our only chance is straight through."

Somehow, the chopper made it to the hospital just outside the base. The jinx had lifted. Ralph Borders suddenly became the luckiest man alive.

After a week and, according to Ralph, "no more than a couple-hundred stitches" at Fairbanks Memorial Hospital, he was flown to Los Angeles where he stayed for two months while undergoing plastic surgery at UCLA Hospital. Grafts from his lower lip were used to reconstruct his upper lip.

By the following spring, with his wounds healed and his firepower beefed up to a .458 Jack Lott Wildcat, Ralph was back bear hunting. In the fall, he hunted moose and ducks. "That bear attack," said his wife, Ellen, "didn't change anything inside."

SLAMMED INTO SUFFOCATION

When you suddenly find yourself stuck between a grizzly and its lunch, it takes supreme audacity to fight back with a battered up little .30/30. And a little luck can't hurt, either.

Roger Stewart's bear first-geared into view, stopped, lowered its head like a bulldozer dropping the blade to wipe out anything in its path, laid its ears back, bristled its neck hair, and lunged.

Roger, who then owned Stewart Archery and Sporting Goods Store in Eagle River, Alaska, was hunting Stone's sheep in British Columbia. He had already taken Dalls and Rocky Mountain bighorns, and the Stone's would be the third animal in his quest for a grand slam with the bow. He had signed on for a two-week hunt with outfitter Coin Collison and Charlie Boya, a Seceney Indian guide.

On the tenth day of the hunt, Roger and Charlie were glassing sheep from about a thousand feet above tree line. Several days before, a local resident had shot one, the offal of which was in rocks about twenty yards above where Roger now sat. He'd discovered the animal remains three days earlier. This day, Charlie climbed up for a fresh look. He called back that something was now "on it."

"What? Birds?"

"Think eagles. Broken rib bones."

It seemed plausible to Roger that eagles could break rib bones. He continued to glass the valley. Charlie then returned, dropped his large canvas pack, laid his old .30/30 rifle on the ground, and decided to walk down the slope to glass from a different vantage point. He'd said he'd call if he saw sheep.

Roger watched as Charlie had walked over a hump, disappeared for a short time in a broad natural trench behind the hump, then come back into view and continued on to a rock outcropping fifty yards away. Seated on the ground, both elbows on his knees, Roger slowly scanned the terrain below with his binoculars. Nothing. He glanced down at Charlie's rifle. A piece of masking tape covered the bore. The tape would keep dirt out of the barrel, but because tape wasn't inside the bore, a bullet would be able to safely pass through. An old sling was wired to the forearm and taped to the shoulder stock. There were no sights, front or back. Charlie had knocked them off because they'd hung up in the scabbard on his horse. It was only a protection firearm, and he was confident that he could sight down the barrel at close range.

Roger returned to glassing. Still nothing. He glanced back down the slope. Charlie was waving frantically.

"He's seen sheep!" Roger thought. He jumped up, put on the pack, and grabbed the rifle with his left hand, the bow with his right.

Ready to go, he glanced back at Charlie again, but now the guide was waving his arms in a pushing motion. "Does he mean don't move?" he wondered, "or has a sheep sneaked up behind me?" He looked back. No sheep. But when he looked forward again, there, just above the crest of the hump, he saw the top of a bear's head bobbing higher and higher with each step until the black-faced, black-footed, blond-bodied grizzly loomed into full view.

Very familiar with bears, Roger immediately grasped the situation. Charlie had walked past the bear at twenty or thirty feet without seeing it. The bear had watched the guide go by, and then got up to go defend its food. Charlie had then looked back at Roger, spotted the bear, and had tried to signal without drawing the bear's attention toward himself. Charlie didn't have so much as a sheath knife for defense. The bear hadn't been running, so it probably wasn't aware of Roger's presence. That didn't help him, of course, because he was trapped between the dead sheep behind him and a 550- to 600-pound bear just thirty feet in front of him.

This was not a confrontation that either party wanted. The bear had not challenged Charlie; it was simply going to protect the food cache in case this human tried to steal it. Roger had never hunted bear, but he knew that a .30/30 is poor short-range defense against a grizzly. Yet, if he stood his ground directly in the bear's path, he would appear to be protecting the dead sheep. If he ran, he would invite a chase-and-attack response. He figured that his only hope was to scare the bear off. "Get out of here!" he had yelled. "Go away!"

The bear stopped, dropped its head, laid its ears back, bristled the hair on its neck, and stared straight at Roger. It would not be bluffed. Roger dropped the bow and shouldered the rifle, cocking the hammer without even wondering whether a cartridge was in the chamber. The bear jumped toward him, hit the ground with a long *ar-r-r-r*, and lunged forward in full charge.

Roger fired at fifteen feet. The bear crumpled slightly, indicating that it felt the jolt, but kept coming. Roger levered another cartridge as he turned to run but was jerked backward off his feet and slammed face down onto the ground.

The bear had grabbed the part of Roger that stuck out farthest and handiest—his big canvas backpack—and hung on now as it tried to right itself to finish the kill. Stewart's 180-grain bullet had apparently broken the bear's right shoulder blade because the bear couldn't stand up on that leg. Each time it tried, its hind feet raised its rump, throwing the bear's weight forward onto Roger's back.

Each time the bear pushed with its three good legs, in its effort to get up, it squeezed all of the air out of Roger's lungs and scooted him a foot or so across the tundra.

Fortunately, pushing with the left leg also shoved the force of the bear's weight onto its own damaged right shoulder. That hurt, so it periodically stopped. But, each time, it would then start all over again.

Every time the bear shoved, Roger lost his air. And with much of the bear's weight always on him, he could never fully gasp the air back before the bear pushed once again. Over and over, with mud and vegetation in his mouth and never time to spit it out before sucking in, he gained a little oxygen, only to immediately lose it again.

In real danger of suffocation, he desperately clung with both hands to the still-cocked rifle under his chest. At last, after scooting Roger ten feet across the tundra, the grizzly couldn't ignore the pain that it was causing to its own damaged shoulder. It rolled back onto its rump, slapping and biting at the wound.

Air came in a rush to Roger as he instantly rolled onto his elbow, pointed the rifle, and fired into the bear at five feet. He had no idea where the bullet struck, but it was effective. The bear rolled over, bawled loudly, stumbled down the slope, and then tumbled over the ledge, perhaps falling as far as a thousand feet before crashing into the alders below.

Roger was still lying on his side when Charlie rushed up, put a hand on his client's shoulder, and said, "Aw, Roger, bad luck, eh? I think he bit your neck." It had certainly looked like that from where Charlie had stood.

Roger felt his neck, brought back a bloody hand, and panicked for a moment. He quickly probed his neck for teeth wounds. "No, I don't think so," he said. "I can't feel anything."

Charlie looked closer. "Oh, he tore my pack!" The bear had never released its grip on the pack until it had rolled off Roger. The blood on his neck was the bear's.

The grizzly was never recovered, nor its death confirmed. The men glassed the area of the fall extensively, but they couldn't climb down that steep rocky face. Roger Stewart was happy to be alive, but not at all pleased about having to shoot a fine animal that he hadn't been hunting.

"I've always felt," he said, "that all of this could have been avoided if I had looked at the dead sheep remains myself. I think I'd have recognized the work of a bear, and the confrontation never would have happened."

NIGHTMARE HUNT

(As told by Rollin Braden)

Rollin Braden struggled for the super resolve it takes to go limp, feign death, and not move a muscle through three savage attacks by two four-hundred-pound brown bears. Now that he achieved it, would he bleed to death before he dared look to see if they had left?

My hunting buddy, Darrel Rosin, chided me as we pushed aside the high brush on the narrow path leading back to the cabin.

"Thought you told me these bears up here go after moose nose like kids after ice cream," he kidded. "Here we've been on this moose hunt for two weeks and nary the sign of a bear. Just doesn't stack up."

Whether we had seen them or not, we were in bear country. It was the tag end of the moose season in southern Alaska, fifty miles south of Soldotna, two hundred miles south of Anchorage.

I was getting anxious about our lack of success as the end of our trip drew near. Finally, my dad, Wes, and my brother, Wayne, managed to get their moose on the same day, but neither Darrel nor I scored.

On one of the last days of our moose hunt, Darrel and I started off through the high willows that surrounded our camp. We had our minds set on adding two more moose carcasses to those already hanging in the tree near the cabin.

Darrel figured that he'd get his from a platform we had built twenty feet up in a tall spruce tree four years earlier. It was a terrific lookout, commanding a splendid view across the thick brush, spruce stands, and tundra bogs.

Darrel let it be known that he was going to get his moose if it took him all day—and it nearly did. At 5:00 P.M., I heard a shot from Darrel's Ruger 77.

"Got him!" I heard him yell. "At one hundred yards." It was a little after 7:00 P.M. when we finished dressing his kill and were starting back to the cabin to stow our meat ax, saw, and rope.

The spruce shadows were, for me, depressingly long. Darrel had gotten his moose, but I was still empty-handed. I was thinking of using up the last half hour or so of twilight to locate a bull that I knew had been with the rest of the bulls we'd taken.

If I couldn't get him tonight, I'd get him at first light tomorrow. Only one day of the season remained.

I stepped just a couple of feet away from Darrel and stopped, listening. Though I couldn't explain it, the silence cloaking the wilderness seemed somehow different. But then, the whole two weeks of September 1985 had been different.

I checked my compass and shoved it in a rear pocket of my hunting pants. I thought to myself that Dad and Wayne were just about finishing their spaghetti dinner a couple of miles down the road at the cabin of our friend, Lou Clarke. I also was thinking how spooky everything seemed out here in the deep twilight and vast wilderness. It was then that I heard a faint rustling in the brush a hundred feet or so away.

"It's your moose," Darrel whispered. "Go get him."

That rustling was almost a summons. That was my moose. I had to get him—now. Somehow I wanted to be alone when I got him.

"Go on ahead," I quietly told Darrel. "I'm going back to meet him. What'll you bet he's a seventy-incher?"

"Shout 'whoopee' when you get him," Darrel said, waving me off and continuing toward the cabin.

Now the adrenaline was flowing through me—but good. I was as anxious and fired up as I had been on previous hunting trips when I got my eight moose. Each year, it seemed, those moments before the kill got increasingly tense and anxious. I cut back the way we had come, angling northward in the direction of the intermittent rustling. Everything seemed fine. I kept low, crouching, on the lookout for anything that moved, testing each step for noise before I shifted my entire weight, and listening for sounds up ahead.

Realizing that the bull might be closer to me than I'd figured earlier, I geared up mentally for sudden action at close range. Another deep and eerie silence settled, and quieting my anxious thoughts wasn't easy. A spine-tingling sensation swept over me—the feeling that whatever I had been watching for in the thick brush up ahead had been, or maybe was, watching me. I didn't dare move fast.

I was waiting for the rustling sound, picturing a hefty bull, a moose with the longed-for seventy-inch rack, a critter far bigger than Dad's or Wayne's or all the eight moose I had taken in other years.

Suddenly, in a sound that came to me like the crack of summer lightning, underbrush snapped a couple of hundred feet away. I stared in the direction of the noise and heard another branch crack, only this time it was much louder. Slowly, just forty feet ahead, I saw the brush beginning to part. My breath stopped in my throat and I gasped as the leaves split apart like a green stage curtain revealing two of the fastest, biggest brown bears I'd ever seen, charging right at me.

"My God!" I heard myself stammer.

In a flash, I took stock. I had a few seconds—no more—to shoot at the half-growling, half-grunting, charging beasts. One was barreling half a length in front of the other. I yelled, but they kept right on coming—their ugly brown faces glistening in the twilight, the rolling fur on their backs undulating like waves on the ocean.

Their enormous jaws were open, revealing rows of huge sharp teeth plainly visible at thirty feet. Their big heads reared up when they saw me, their tongues hanging out. They neither hesitated nor slowed down. There was no time now for fear or paralysis. Each bear must have been several feet tall, weighing four hundred pounds or more. In that split second, they looked to me like monsters from outer space.

It is amazing how much agility comes with reflex in a life-or-death situation. I whirled to the right, hoping that my .338-caliber Ruger 77 would do the job.

I shot from the waist. The crack of my rifle seemed to reverberate for miles. I stared ahead, astounded that nothing had changed. Both glaring bears were still charging toward me. I'm a crack shot, but this time, when it really mattered, I missed. The bullet hit a tree.

Now, plainly visible were the ugly yellow spikes of teeth protruding from drooling jaws. I froze. Time seemed to stop, and I remember glancing at the beasts' claws for just a split second ahead of realizing they'd be on me before I could chamber another round. I spun on my heels; now my back was to them and I was braced for their first blows. I dropped my rifle and threw my hands over my face, protecting my eyes. As I did this, the bears lunged. I felt a staggering blow against my back and then a force, like a team of linebackers, struck my shoulders, knocking me down. Sharp sticks cut my lips and weeds jammed in my mouth. My nose and forehead were wedged flat against the forest moss. Then, a ton of weight, like the wheels of a car, pinned down my back. I could hear strange, thick, guttural animal sounds and the sound of spasmodic breathing.

What I decided then was wrong—I know it now, but I wasn't thinking clearly at the time. I had been thrashing my arms and legs, but it suddenly occurred to me that my struggle was futile. "Why fight?" I asked myself. "You're dead already. Why resist?" At that moment, one of the bears started chewing my ear after knocking my cowboy hat off.

Something in me advised: play dead. Bears are supposed to get disinterested and leave. But you've got to lie perfectly still. "Still? How?" a voice within me screamed. I jammed my thumbs down into the earth as the first of countless agonizing spikes began piercing my buttocks and up and down my spine. Now, the slashing attack moved higher.

Horror swept me as I felt pressure, like a foot, near my ear. Then the real agony—I felt one of the beasts yanking my head up to get a better grip on my neck. Stifling a scream, I ground my mouth into the earth.

The grating sound intensified. Instead of letting up, the bears became more ferocious. My entire body was being shoved and shaken with tremendous animal power. My knees were being stomped and ground down into the brush. One of the beasts was working on my back, the other on my skull. Then, they traded places. The sequence of events is hard to sort out, though. My mental pictures of the agony are mercifully blurred.

The most horrible sensations came when they began gnawing at my head. I had a mental image of one of the bears clamping its open jaw around the entire top of my head, attempting to crush in the bones, but not quite succeeding. I heard the animals panting in my ears. I figured that I was in the throes of death. Death from bleeding. Death from shock.

I fought to keep from moving or twitching. Something in me seemed to be ordering me to lie still, motionless, but my body rebelled and my left leg twitched sharply. Every time there was movement, it was followed by a burst of more spikes of shooting pain.

They chewed on my head and back for what seemed hours, or days. Then they stopped abruptly to rest. I sprawled absolutely motionless and silent, my heart thumping wildly. I could feel my pulse pounding in my wrists and temples.

"Lie still," I warned myself. "Don't move. You've lost a lot of blood. Try to run and they'll flatten you and finish the job. If you as much as twitch, you're done for."

I stiffened my knees to hold them firm, but the effort brought movement that instantly caught the bears' attention and brought both of them roaring to a standing position. Then they settled back and I could see them several yards away, their pig-like eyes glaring at me.

Miraculously, I was still alive—but for how long? How many arteries and blood vessels can rupture before you bleed to death? How many slashes can you take and still remain perfectly motionless?

Somehow, it comforted me to think about what I had been told all my life: bears will gulp down fresh moose, but you can count on most of them leaving without completely devouring the remains of a man. Sometimes, they return to cover the meat with leaves and twigs, but they go away for days until decomposition progresses to a certain stage. Because bears relish rancid meat, some attack victims have revived enough to climb out of the debris and survive.

I'll never forget the wave of relief and thankfulness that swept over me when the creatures were no longer on my back, jabbing and pulling.

"Are they gone?" a voice inside me asked. "Look and see."

Saliva clogged my mouth and throat. Slowly, I turned my head to the left. My face was caked with blood-soaked dirt, so I wiped my eyes and tried to look into the distance. That was all those waiting bears needed. Roaring, they were back at me, pouncing with new ferocity. One of them clamped its fangs on my shoulder, sending sharp teeth deep into muscle as pain zigzagged down my side, down my leg, to my toes. Now they began in earnest to rip the flesh at the back of my skull.

Despite the intense pain, the only thing on my mind was an image of my children.

"God, let me live," I begged. "I want to see Max and Melinda again."

Things seemed to go blank for a moment and the scene wavered. Then, as if I were detached from the horror now enveloping me, a part of me began lecturing to the other part. I heard myself say, "Go limp . . . repeat over and over: I am still, still as death. I will let them chew. I will not move . . . I will play dead . . . play dead . . . let it happen . . . let them have me . . ."

"I can't," a part of me resisted.

"Yes, you can. Repeat: I will let them chew. I will not move. I will play dead." My inner voice seemed to be repeating the admonitions over and over.

I don't know how many minutes or seconds this eerie confab went on. I had long since lost track of how much time had passed. Tremors of pain were cutting into my chest now. A new and terrible fear seized me as the bears moved from my back to other parts of my body and alongside my lungs.

Then, in one moment, all of life seemed to ebb and stand still. Gone was the slurping, pulling, grunting, crunching, licking. Silence. Dead silence. "How," I wondered, "can something so huge move off so fast and so silently?"

But I knew they were nearby, sitting only yards away, their eyes watching for the slightest movement, their ears tensed for the slightest sound from my body. I forced myself not to look, not to raise my head, not to move so much as a finger or an eyelash. Now, all was deep, agonizing silence. Nothing moved. From my limbs, neck, and face, blood seeped silently into the dirt. My body seemed frozen, glued down, a part of the earth. Motionless, I listened. Now there was no rustling, no footsteps, no dry twigs breaking. Do I dare raise my head now, I wondered, or will they come at me again?

I kept my eyes closed tight and a kind of peace filtered through the pain. I saw the little church that I attended in Soldotna. I saw my dad and mom. I saw my sister, JoAnn, and my brothers. I was with them and, suddenly, somehow, I got the courage to lift my head just a little bit so I could look around.

The bears were gone. But how far? Were they lurking just behind that clump of spruce trees, ready to charge again? I had no idea where the bears were, but I told myself that, if they came back, I'd let them finish me off and end my suffering. I didn't want any more of that awful pain. But they weren't around, and somehow I had to find the strength to get away.

"Try getting up," I told myself. "See if you can stand without falling." Was I brain-damaged in the attack? I had to be able to think. If a lot of my brain was gone, would I be rational? Could I trust my thinking?

Fighting back the pain, I somehow was able to get on my feet. I realized then that my legs hadn't been broken. I lifted my hands to feel my head. My hand slid under my scalp as under a hat. I took my binoculars off over my head, unbuttoned my wool shirt with one hand, and slipped down my suspenders to strip off my shirt. There was no way I could let go of my head and remove my shirt without the loosened skin sliding out of place.

"I've got to get out of here fast," I kept thinking. "But which way?" New blood poured down my cheeks, soaking my pants and shirt.

Despite all this, I felt no revulsion, just an aching hope that somehow I might get my shirt tied around my head to hold everything in place until I could get help. I could see partially, but every movement I made seemed to increase the bleeding and to bring on greater weakness.

All the trees looked the same. "Show me which way to go," I prayed. "Help me to choose the right direction."

Maybe, I thought, the bears are still lurking around.

"Help me," I muttered aloud. "Help me." Then I yelled, "Darrel! Darrel! Help."

I started to run, to this day I don't know how, but I pushed the tall grass aside, stumbling, screaming. "Darrel! Help!"

Darrel heard my yelling. He cut back into the woods in the direction of my voice and then stopped dead in his tracks.

"Oh my God!" he exclaimed as he saw me.

I thought he was going to faint, but he helped me back to the cabin. Dad and Wayne were there when we arrived.

Someone gave me a mirror. I couldn't believe that the awfully mangled creature I saw was me. The entire back of my head, ear to ear, had been opened and lifted. The scalp was falling to the front like a slipped wig. A piece of scalp was missing. Punctures in my shoulder were so deep that I thought my lungs might be pierced. My back and legs were covered with gashes and bites. The bears' teeth had punctured through more than three inches of buttocks flesh. My head had been chewed badly. Sticks, grass, dirt, and bear saliva were in the wounds. My favorite watch, the one I liked because it was thin and easy on the hunt, was crunched through the dial. It had stopped at exactly 7:33 P.M.

Working swiftly, Darrel made a tourniquet out of a towel and tightened it around my head. Dad, meanwhile, cleaned the blood from my face and body.

The guys flung a mattress into the trailer and I climbed in. The trailer was hooked onto our four-wheeler. By now, the pain was beginning to break through my consciousness as the protecting shock wore away.

Wayne was driving, and he frantically spun the wheels in his haste to get us out of the cabin and through the woods to our pickup truck parked six miles away. Once we got to the truck, we would drive sixty miles to Soldotna, where there would be a doctor and a plane to take me to Providence Hospital in Anchorage, two hundred miles away.

The white bath towel that the guys had given me had turned bright red. The pain in one of my buttocks was so great that I shifted my body in the trailer. It was too much effort to reach into my wool pants pocket to see what was jabbing me whenever we hit a bump. (I later found out that it was a chewing tobacco can.)

Conversation was sparse as we drove to the pickup truck. Darrel seemed to be feeling guilty about having not responded when he heard my shout and the shot I fired. But, at the time, Darrel thought that I had gotten my moose and was yelling "whoopee."

"I was so happy for you," he said. "I threw my hat in the air and hollered, 'Yiiieee! Another moose bit the dust.' If only I had known."

What none of us knew was that more surprises were still in store. We got to the pickup only to find that we had to change a flat tire. Our troubles continued at the airline counter in Soldotna. There were no planes in the airport, so one was ordered to be flown out of Anchorage.

I arrived in the emergency room of Providence Hospital at 3:00 A.M. My physician, Dr. Jim Scully of Anchorage, spent five hours applying two hundred stitches and flushing and picking pine needles from my skull.

Rollin Braden spent eight days in the hospital, four of them in intensive care. He recovered from the ordeal in record time and without disfigurement.

BEAR IN CAMP

(As told by Bob Herron)

City living had conditioned Bob Herron to call for services. Doing it yourself could even get you into trouble. Would Bob have the considerable courage to reverse his usual behavior, take charge when the fishing guide didn't, and face a giant bear with a little .357 Colt?

"Bear! Bear! Bear!" shattered the silence just before dawn. I grabbed my .357 Colt on the second "Bear!" and was nearly out of the tent by the third. The screaming yell came from the cook, who was the wife of the guide and daughter of the outfitter. The tone of her voice rose from initial surprise through warning to sheer terror.

"He was a big one," breathed her cousin as the others arrived from their tents. Up from the Lower Forty-eight for the summer, the cousin was acting as general assistant around camp. He had seen the bear first. He heard the bear smash the cooler, break up the barbecue grill, and rip the rubber boat. And he watched it run away.

The bear was a wilderness Alaska brown, one of the giant coastal bears that evolved over eons without threat from any creature. They learned to regard the world as theirs to plunder. Although they don't normally consider man a meal, it's never wise to get in the way of their quick-tempered, unbending determination to have what they want, when they want it.

Before our fishing trip in August 1986, I had been concerned enough about bears to ask the outfitter whether we should bring firearms. He wrote, "You don't need them, but it can't hurt to have them." Firearms are worthless, or worse, unless you're confident in their use, of course, so my wife, Marietta, Bill Myers, and I practiced at a pistol range prior to departing Southern California. My thought right after that visit from the bear at 4:00 A.M. was, "Well, so far the outfitter is right. We didn't need the firearms." I hoped that would remain correct. And if the bear became more aggressive, I hoped the guide would take care of the matter. He had a Remington .30-06 semiautomatic rifle. He was the paid professional, wasn't he?

With only an hour until dawn, and a marauding bear out there somewhere in the dark, none of us went back to bed. But at 5:00 A.M., with the Monday morning sun silhouetting mountains in the east, the world seemed a safer place. We seven paying guests, five men and two women, were, after all, in Alaska to fish for salmon in the Tsiu River for a week, not to worry about bears. The Tsiu split into wandering fingers through the delta of glacier-ground sand several hundred yards wide before entering the Gulf of Alaska. The salmon were eager to slash at three-inch silver spoons studded with fake salmon eggs, and the cook performed magic with fish in the cook tent.

I was casting hip-deep in water 150 yards from camp and thinking about the previous day. A six-passenger floatplane had flown my group of five within two miles of camp, but then a little two-passenger aircraft ferried us the rest of the way in relays because the water surrounding our island camp wasn't expansive enough for larger planes to land. Two other guests arrived later in the day. Four high wall tents were pitched over wooden floors and plywood walls. A fifth tent was being built when we arrived. In the small amount of time left for fishing that day, we had taken six large silver salmon.

The recollection of those six fish brought me back to the bear. We had cleaned the salmon, tied them in a plastic bag, and submerged the whole thing in the water to keep the fish cool. The bag was held in place with a cord tied around a stick that was shoved into the sand behind the tent where Marietta, Bill, and I slept. I shuddered slightly at the thought that this enormous animal had fished those salmon out of the water and had eaten them, plastic bag and all. And the bear had done it so silently that we never heard him just ten feet away. Obviously, I made a serious mistake when I staked those fish behind the tent. If a bear's sense of smell is keen enough to locate salmon from the small amount of scent that leaks out of a tightly tied and submerged plastic bag, having any kind of fish in camp is like waving a welcome sign at a bear. I puzzled over why the guide hadn't warned us not to do it.

Hardly anyone talked about fishing when we broke for lunch on the second day. Marietta hadn't caught a thing, probably because she wasn't concentrating on fishing. She gave it up for the day. The bear kept coming up in our conversation. He was a big one, the camp assistant had said. How big is a big bear when you're talking about an Alaska brown? Would the bear return? Would he attack? Privately each of us wondered what he or she would, should, or should not do if the bear did come back. The guide, in his few words, tried to calm our fears and urged us to forget the bear and simply enjoy the fishing.

That afternoon, the outfitter flew in with more building materials for the fifth tent. We crowded around him, excitedly telling of our experience with the bear and expressing our fears about its return. Finally, the outfitter looked at all of us and said, "Well, you may have to do away with that bear."

That stunned me—not that we might have to kill the bear if it became a menace, but that the outfitter looked at all of us when he said it. I didn't say anything, but my thoughts were, "You kill the bear, or tell the guide to kill the bear. I paid to come here and fish."

It took days before I recognized that the outfitter and I were conditioned by different worlds. In the Los Angeles suburb where I live, if the plumbing leaks, you call the plumber. If the street caves in, you call the city. You don't fix it yourself. There's a guy either elected or paid to do almost everything. In fact, you'd make trouble for yourself if you tried to do a lot of things yourself. But in camp, if we wanted a fire, we looked for the wood. It was expected we would take care of ourselves. On the frontier, or the recent frontier, people are, by necessity, self-reliant and self-sufficient. If the bear becomes a problem, the outfitter seemed to be saying, it's up to everyone to help solve that problem.

That evening, the guide did stake our cleaned fish about two hundred yards from camp. Too late, I thought, but again, I didn't say it. He seemed like a nice young man, quiet and probably still in his twenties. Maybe he felt awkward about giving orders to considerably older people. But I suspected that the bear would be back in camp again to look for fish because he had found some there the first time.

At dinner, bear talk once more almost obliterated fishing tales, despite the guide's terse attempt to assure us that everything would be all right. It was not all right with Marietta. "We should have a bear watch tonight," she insisted. "We shouldn't let the bear get that close again without knowing about it." The guide seemed very annoyed when we agreed with Marietta and counted the guns in camp. We made a rule: no one would drink on watch.

It wasn't quite dark in the long northern twilight when, at about 10:30 P.M., the bear was sighted crossing shallow water in the slough two hundred yards from camp. All of us were jumpy. No one was in bed. We all ran out, yelling and clanging pots and pans. When the bear left, the guide resumed grumbling that a bear watch was unnecessary. "It's okay," Marietta told him. "Go to bed. Bill and I will stay up." But he stayed with them. So did the camp assistant, who borrowed a .44 Magnum single-action Ruger revolver from another California guest. Marietta and I had .357 Colts, and Bill had a .357 Smith & Wesson.

Rain made it an uncomfortable watch, but the bear was sighted at 12:30 A.M. in the moonlight during a lull in the downpour. Everyone was back up, yelling and banging. The bear returned again at 2:00 A.M. and came closer—between fifty and seventy-five yards. It was getting harder to chase him off by screaming and banging. The guards retired after daybreak at about 5:30 A.M.

That morning, Tuesday, a group of Anchorage residents flew in by chartered plane for a day's salmon fishing. "What are all of you fellows carrying around on your hips?" one of them asked me, "and what for?"

I told him that mine was a .357, and I explained about the brown bear.

"If a brown bear attacks, the best thing you can do with a .357," he said, "is stick it in your mouth and pull the trigger. Killing a brown bear with a .357 is like trying to knock down a bowling pin with a marble."

That was the first time I heard that a .357 is not an adequate weapon against Alaska browns. Later, I read a quote by Sergeant Bob Brown of the Alaska Department of Public Safety: "We don't have any authenticated reports where any lives were saved from brown bear attacks by using a handgun. There have been times when an attacking bear has been killed by a handgun, but the individual was also killed." I was unnerved. If the bear attacked, our only hope now seemed to be the guide's .30-06. Marietta completely withdrew from fishing. Tuesday night, the cook replaced Bill on watch. Marietta stayed up again, too. At 1:00 A.M., fog rolled in, and everyone went to bed. It's strangely deceitful the way fog closes in around us and almost cuddles us into the illusion of comfortable safety. It was no struggle for Leico, however, to regain her wariness, even in fog. She got up at 2:30 A.M., found no one on watch, and stayed up. Leico and Paul Whitestone, the other two Californians in our party, were recent acquaintances. Paul seemed unworried about the bear, confident that the guide would handle it. His calm even showed in his fishing. Bill and I were catching six to eight salmon a day; Paul was catching ten to fourteen. His calm, however, left his wife all the more nervous. Paul had lent his .44 Magnum revolver to the camp assistant but kept a relatively ineffective .38 Special for their own protection, and their tent was on the vulnerable fringe of camp.

At 4:00 A.M., Leico was banging on a garbage can. The fog had lifted and the bear was back, this time from the brush to the east. We rolled out in time to see the bear stand up fifty yards away in the beam of our flashlight. The great bear swung his head back and forth, scenting us. Thank goodness I brought a six-cell flashlight. The only other flashlights in camp were little two-cells. The bear dropped down on all fours and came within thirty yards of a tent occupied by a very sick elderly gentleman and his son. I fired three shots into the air to frighten the bear and others did the same. Bill shot twice. Marietta said that four other shots were touched off before the bear left.

By Wednesday, fishing for most of us was just something to do until the bear returned. There was no radio in camp, so we could not communicate with the outside; otherwise, some of us would have called for a plane to fly us out of there right away. The bear was getting bolder, and I didn't know how long we could keep frightening him off. Finally, I asked the guide, “How do you know when it’s time to shoot the bear?”

“You’ll know,” he answered.

“That doesn’t tell me much.”

The subject was dropped right there with a long silent look at each other.

I went to bed early. Bill and the camp assistant took the first watch. With both moonlight and the aurora borealis, it was bright enough to see the bear cross a little inlet 150 yards to the south. Bill fired into the air, and the bear picked up speed but didn’t change direction. He was headed for two Alaska Department of Fish and Game biologists who were camped two or three miles to the south. One of them told us later that the bear pawed and sniffed outside their tent, doubly terrifying the younger man, who was just as afraid of his handgun as he was of the bear. He hadn’t fired a handgun before. The men made noise but didn’t go outside the tent and didn’t shoot. Finally, the bear left.

At around 1:00 A.M., Bill came into the tent. “I’m going to bed,” he said. “The assistant is still up.” I felt that one person on watch finds it not only frightening but also lonely and needs moral support. I got up. At least with two people, the time would seem to pass more quickly.

At about 2:00 A.M., I saw the bear silhouetted by the moonlight on the vast sand flat to the west. He was seventy yards away and on the other side of a finger of the river that was only fifteen yards wide and three feet deep. I jumped, screamed at the bear, and fired two shots into the air. The bear ignored me and kept coming at a fast trot.

Everyone piled out of the tents. The bear was now directly across the shallow slough just fifteen yards away. Should we quickly build up the fire and stay near it? We decided that we wouldn’t be able to see the bear as well with a bright light between us. We stood behind a log at the water’s edge, firing warning shots and trying to reload in the dark. The cook was on top of the log with the six-cell flashlight. I glanced at her. She was trembling. The bear was trotting back and forth, trying to make up his mind.

There was no question in my mind about the bear's intentions. After all of our noisy efforts to run him off, if he came across the water, I knew he wouldn't hesitate to kill us to get what he wanted from what he considered his home territory. By then, maybe he was angry enough about being kept out that *we* were what he wanted. We had to do something while there was still time.

The water would slow the bear and give us a decent shot. If he got across, he'd be so fast on land that we wouldn't have a chance. "This is it," I yelled. "No more warning shots. Marietta, keep your gun in reserve in case he gets across. If he's on me and I can't use my gun, stick it in his ear and shoot."

The bear stood, drew one front paw up and waved his massive head from side to side to test our scent. "If he comes," I yelled again, "shoot to kill." Then I shut up and tried to calm myself. The first time I hunted deer, I shot once and then jacked all of the other cartridges through the chamber and onto the ground without pulling the trigger. I couldn't afford buck fever now.

The bear dropped to all fours. Down the little two-foot bank he came and into the water. Bill fired two quick shots. I fired once when the bear's back was exposed as he went down the bank. I expected to hear a barrage, and I especially wanted to hear the .30 06. "Oh, damn" the guide said, and I never heard the rifle. Marietta turned to see what was wrong. The guide pulled the trigger again, trying to get the .30-06 to fire.

Bill fired again. Neither the camp assistant nor Paul shot. Apparently, they were frozen by shock. Leico was crying. The bear turned broadside in the shallow water. "Don't shoot," the guide yelled, "He's not wounded. I saw the bullets hit the water."

It was too late. I had already pulled the trigger too far to stop the shot. The bear was turning to its left to quarter away. I couldn't see my sights in the moonlight, but the revolver was pointing at the whole bear in the flashlight beam. The muzzle flash was almost blinding, yet I saw the bear flinch and his hind legs jerk.

Because the guide had told us not to shoot, I hesitated and lost the chance to empty my gun into the bear. I was immediately angry with myself for that. If neither Bill nor I had hit the bear, it would come back to terrify us, as it had every night. If the bear was wounded, he could be a determined killer. I was certain that I had hit the bear at least once.

With nearly three hours of darkness remaining, all of us were hyper. We looked out over the sand flat in the direction the bear went, but worried that he might come in from behind us. The guide checked the cartridge that hadn't gone off. The primer wasn't dented enough to fire the cartridge. That's common with guns that aren't cleaned thoroughly.

The cook stood up on the log. "There he goes," she yelled. "See him? Running to the south!"

I thought I saw him about three hundred yards out. So did Marietta and Bill. Leico didn't say anything. Paul asked Bill for a cigarette. Then, the bear was gone.

For the second time, the cook expressed her fear of all guns. Someone could get shot if the bear came at us from an unexpected direction. "Just calm down," the guide said, which was the only realistic response to that.

During the long wait for daylight, we sighted the bear several times moving in the distance. Usually the cook saw him first. She seemed to have the keenest eyes.

At daybreak, nothing was moving. We were trying to decide what to do—stay where we were or track the wounded bear. Then Bill, through his binoculars, saw an unfamiliar lump on the sand about 150 yards away. Thinking it could be the bear, Bill and the guide waded across the slough and soon found a stripe of bear dung on the sand that pointed toward the lump.

The bear was dead. When it was skinned, only two bullets were found. One .357 bullet had hit the right rear leg and then ranged down along the bone to a point below the knee. The killing .357 had hit high in the right rib cage, almost at the last rib, and then ranged forward through a lung to a point between the front legs. It lodged just beneath the skin.

All five shots fired at the bear came from Bill's revolver or mine. He had a Smith & Wesson, and I had a Colt. We have those bullets, and we know by its deformed shape which bullet did the killing. We constantly tease each other and joke about who made the killing shot. Of course, close examination of the bullet would reveal who killed the bear. Colt and Smith & Wesson rifling systems differ, and examination of the rifling grooves on the base of the fatal bullet would tell us whose revolver had fired it. But we avoid making the investigation because arguing about the kill is so much fun. Perhaps we still need some comic relief.

At about 3:30 on the afternoon after the bear was killed, a plane flew in with supplies. We were in great spirits by then, almost giddy with relief. All of us were chattering at once when we told the pilot about our experience. Suddenly, he said, "About a mile from here, I spooked another big bear with the plane."

You could almost feel a shock wave in the sudden silence. "Good God," I said at last, "is it going to start all over again?"

"Have you got any room in the plane for passengers?" Marietta asked. "I don't like to be in the same train wreck twice." I went too.

Sure enough, we saw the bear. The pilot flew very low over it several times, trying to chase it away from camp.

WHO WILL BE THE SACRIFICIAL LAMB?

It would take superhuman effort for three men to disobey their brain stem flight commands when the bear attacked, and little Lani knew she'd be left behind. Yet so far the men were keeping their wits.

Excitement filled the air as four Seattle adventurers stepped off the tour boat *Thunder Bay*. A boatload of mostly Japanese tourists waved, snapped pictures, and shook their heads in disbelief—casting the Seattle four in the role of intrepid explorers. Little did they know.

For these seasoned outdoor people, however, stepping off onto a sandbar at Wolf Point in Alaska's Glacier Bay National Park was only a touristy add-on. Their main adventure, so they thought, had started with hiking the arduous thirty-three-mile Chilkoot Trail that took so many gold miners' lives in 1898. From Lake Bennett, they canoed to the headwaters of the Yukon River and on to Whitehorse, a total of ninety miles, trolling baits and feasting on trout along the way.

They would now camp and explore the receding glacier at White Thunder Ridge. It would be two rather tame days. Persistent rains seemed the greatest challenge. But somehow, the tourists' send-off gave them a feeling of commitment—perhaps in part because they knew that twenty-five-year-old Alan Lee Precup, a lone camper from Aurora, Illinois, did not meet the tour boat as scheduled two days earlier.

Oldest of the four, Dr. Charles Jackson, then thirty-one and a research fellow at the University of Washington, strongly felt that ground search crews should have been out the next day. Instead, the National Park Service waited for an aerial search, and bad weather delayed that another day. Charles reasoned that instead of causing a delay, bad weather should have prompted an immediate search. Precup could be injured, perhaps die from exposure.

Dr. Peter Talbot, thirty, a resident at Children's Hospital, agreed, as did Lani Vega, his girlfriend. Lani had spent several years growing up on Alaska's Kodiak Island. Peter had worked, fished, and hunted for several years at Ketchikan. Colin Miller, twenty-six, was an accomplished outdoorsman and a research fellow with a psychology degree. All planned to look for Precup as they hiked and explored.

One other governmental faux pas caught their attention. At the bottom of their Forest Service topography map, they were advised to carry firearms in the wilderness. On this same piece of real estate, at the time, the Park Service denied the public that right.

Just as the Seattle group was leaving the boat, two others, Karen from Florida and Marv from Vermont, decided to join them. Charles was rather impressed with Karen. Although he was very perceptive, articulate, and often the group's spokesman, his observations temporarily went no further than this slender girl's long blond hair and dark, penetrating eyes.

Peter was much less impressed. He was hearing a girl with a take-charge attitude based on far too little outdoor experience as a volunteer assistant park ranger. She had picked up all the most seriously flawed stereotypical ranger attitudes: "Park visitors are always inexperienced and ignorant." "Understanding the natural world automatically comes with the uniform." "Wearing the uniform bestows membership in an in-the-know, us-against-them tribe that works best if associating with other members." And worst of all, "If you're nice to large predators, they'll always be nice back."

Up from bedrock shoreline, White Thunder Ridge rises fourteen hundred feet above Muir Inlet, running east and west on the five-mile peninsula. Its north side drops vertically to the inlet. Glacial ice partially covers the south side. The group hiked inland for about an hour to the first set of small lakes. Here, they decided to set up camp, eat lunch, and then hike to the glacier.

Karen decided that she and Marv would forego lunch, pitch a tent at the next little lake, and then go on ahead. They would all meet later at the glacier.

By 11:30 A.M. the Seattle group was eating, looking around at the deglaciated area, and preparing for the hike. At one time, ice had scraped down the bedrock, leaving behind yards of silt-to-gravel-sized glacial till in places. Washouts formed dips and ravines in the landscape. Thick stands of four- to eight-foot alders grew in slashes of till. Low, browned-off ground cover appeared to be the only other growth. Nothing they saw seemed capable of supporting wildlife. Colin stuck an ice ax in his belt to help negotiate the glacier.

Suddenly, Peter saw a bear a hundred yards away on the opposite side of the little lake. It didn't seem threatening, so they snapped a few pictures. But it kept coming their way. Charles and Lani walked forty feet toward the bear, banging pots. The bear slowed, and then disappeared into the alders, popping up here and there, finally only thirty-five yards away.

Peter and Colin decided to move the food to avoid a destroyed camp and two hungry days before the tour boat returned. Nobody felt great fear at this point, but everyone hurried north and circled up a ridge to gain a vantage point to watch the bear. Despite the absence of food, they saw the animal, easily identifiable as an Alaskan coastal brown bear, savagely shredding camp.

Peter and Colin found a steep cliff, tied rope to rock, and lowered the food. By now the bear had left camp, slowly and methodically, nose to the ground, trailing the campers. Several times it disappeared into the alders, only to reappear much closer each time. The group hurried back toward camp, deliberately circling the small lake to keep it between them and the advancing bear. Their camp was destroyed. Torn tents were rolled into balls.

Park Service had said there were no bears in this area. Indeed, there was nothing on this rock and glacial ice to support large predators. Yet, here was a bear. And it trailed past the food cache without paying the slightest attention. By now the group was having strong suspicions about what had happened to Alan Precup.

To Lani, it was a childhood nightmare coming true. On Kodiak Island, a pursuing bear had haunted her sleep. Now she was thinking about survival of the fittest. At five feet, ninety-five pounds, and female, she was keenly aware of being the smallest, weakest, slowest, most easily caught member of the group.

With no support equipment left in camp, nothing but one ice ax and four pocketknives for defense, thirty to forty miles from the lodge, and the bear still patiently following their trail, retreat remained their only option. Once again they headed north around the small lake and up to an elevation of seven hundred feet. Perhaps they could find a cliff steep enough to defend by rolling rocks down on the bear.

Pace quickened. The bear ignored the camp this time. Still trailing, it disappeared into the alders. Everyone tried to run within fifty feet of each other while slipping and sliding up the difficult erosion fingers of glacial till that fanned out from the ridge. They were becoming winded. Jackets, sweaters, and ponchos were shed. And still no defendable site could be seen.

Colin was running below a rock outcropping about a third of the way up a gravel knoll when the bear crashed out of the alders and splashed through a small kettle pond. It was running head high and fast, obviously following the airborne scent of overheated humans. It disappeared into a ravine behind the alders. Colin raced to the top of the knoll where the others were arriving from the opposite side of the outcropping.

Lani was running second behind Peter. Charles consciously hung back in a chivalrous attempt to protect Lani from being the last and most vulnerable. Suddenly, the bear loped out of the alders. "Chuck, he's close," Peter yelled. "Get up here!"

Charles glanced back. The bear was fifty feet away. Instantly, he found himself racing past Lani. All of the accumulated cultural civility in his cerebral cortex had been short-circuited by a flight command right out of the primitive brain stem. Lani was too terrified to notice.

At the top of the mound, nobody had the wind or energy to run farther. The four clustered, not only for safety in numbers, but to offer the appearance of a larger adversary.

The bear, mouth open, slobbering, and giving its full attention to air scent as it ran, appeared not to see the humans. They shouted, wildly waving their arms. Suddenly aware of how close it was to this now formidable-looking group, the bear locked all four legs and, almost cartoonlike, skidded to a stop in the gravel. He was ten feet away, just across a small gully.

The bear paced back and forth, looking for a weak spot. Somebody suggested that Lani would be safer behind them and a bit down the back side of the crest. Already feeling that she was still alive only because she was with a group, Lani quickly complied.

Although a member of the world's largest bear species, a giant relative of the grizzly, this coastal brown bear appeared scrawny, not much over six hundred pounds. Its cinnamon coat was scraggly. It was probably a youngster pushed out to find its own territory and starving on this mostly barren peninsula.

The bear continued to pace back and forth as an outnumbered predator might, intimidating the herd, biding its time, waiting for an individual to lose nerve and bolt.

In a highly individualistic demonstration, the men began yelling at the bear. Colin had practiced roaring like a lion in acting classes. He made bestial noises. Peter became rational, rather academic with the bear. Charles swore up a storm. Lani was quiet, calling no attention to herself.

The bear was unimpressed. It noiselessly paced and waited, eyes always on the group. "Well," Charles observed, "we have cameras. At least they'll know what happened to us." He began shooting pictures.

Colin, holding the ice ax, became very agitated. At times, perhaps out of fear, he actually wished the bear would make its move and get it over with. A conversation ensued about what was the most vulnerable spot on a bear. The pineal gland, deep within the brain—but how do you get an ice ax or pocketknife though a skull that thick? Try for the heart behind the left leg? The spine in the neck?

For the time, they had a plan. Colin held the ice ax. He would be the first line of defense. If he fell, he would toss it to the next nearest person. It was all very unworkable, though. While they hoped to rationalize a solution through all of this talking, it was also a way of psychologically extracting themselves from the dilemma.

The bear kept pacing, menacingly searching for an opening. Rocks! Throw rocks! Won't that trigger an attack? What else is there? Lani marveled at how the men were keeping their wits about them. But she didn't necessarily agree with agitating the bear. If it charged, everyone would scatter. She would be left behind.

It was easy to hit the bear at ten feet. Several rocks struck the body. Lani saw it stand up. Colin had a two-pound rock in his hand. Hard as he could throw, he struck the bear squarely on the end of its snout. It dropped to all fours, sniffed, pawed at its nose, then walked off uphill about fifty feet and sat down on a flat rock.

Elevated ten feet higher than the people, the bear continued its vigil. Eventually, it lay down. But every time someone moved, up came its head. By now, it was 2:30 P.M. They had been chased for two and a half hours and pinned down for another thirty minutes. The men felt they had achieved a temporary standoff, but trying to leave would likely instigate an attack.

"We can't stay here, either," someone observed. "He'll pick us off at will after dark."

More rationalizing: "If only there were trees. Most grizzlies can't climb." "It's cooling off, and there's no way to retrieve our clothing. No way to outrun a bear." "If we can just get down to the water, the bear probably won't swim after us." "We wouldn't swim long, either," someone added. From their seven-hundred-foot elevation, they could see the inlet—and the startlingly blue icebergs floating by.

And then thoughts too terrible to think crept from their brains and onto their tongues. It was a final, desperate attempt of human minds to bring hope through logic to a horribly irrational situation. Yet, the thoughts were so repulsive that the survivors could couch memories of them only in such personally disassociated terms as "it was said," or "we talked about." No one said "I thought," or "he suggested," and nobody now recalls who said it first, but it had been on the minds of all four. Logic suggested that if the bear attacked, it would stay with the first person caught long enough to allow others to escape.

"Sacrifice" was too terrible to say. And finally, the men decided it would not happen. They would not split and run. They would stand together against the bear. But down deep, each wondered—not run from a charging bear? Lani was silent. Everyone had already run from the bear, and she had been last in line. She knew she would be the sacrifice.

"Bears don't like fires," Colin said. But the vegetation was wet from continual rains. Nothing could be dried enough to ignite with their few matches and several pieces of paper from wallets. Talbot, especially, kept thinking how foolish it was to be unarmed in the wilderness.

In the meantime, Karen and Marv were wondering why the group hadn't joined them as planned. Walking back toward camp, they heard the yelling. Approaching within a quarter mile, they could see the bear and the people.

Karen began her own yelling, joined by Marv, to inform the others how stupid they were for having "chased the bear up the hill." In her sidewalk outdoor education, it was politically correct to blame humans for any animal/human confrontation. Karen, therefore, did not think to question how an animal capable of thirty-five miles an hour could be chased down by four humans. Neither did she wonder why an animal with the size and temperament of a coastal brown would remain "chased up the hill" instead of fighting back or simply walking off.

At that moment, hope appeared in the sky—an old two-seater search plane looking for Alan Precup. The Seattle group frantically flagged the plane, hoping the pilot would buzz the bear. The plane circled and wagged its wings. The group was elated.

Karen was now angrily shouting to stop flagging the plane. They were interrupting the search for Precup.

But the trapped group's flagging was useless anyway. The pilot, it turned out, had not seen the bear and the four people. He had, however, sighted Karen and Marv approaching the camp, which from his altitude didn't appear torn up. Assuming everything was fine, he merely wagged his wings in greeting, and flew away.

While yelling, Karen did impart one useful piece of information. She and Marv had observed a boat in the bay bringing ground search personnel ashore. Safety was three-quarters of a mile away—if they could get there without provoking an attack. Indeed, the addition of two more people shouting back and forth had seemed to make a difference to the bear. Instead of impatiently alerting to every move, jerking its head or standing up, it lay there quietly watching.

The group decided to risk leaving their knoll. The bear clearly took notice, but did not move. Watching over their shoulders, they slowly inched through the low cover. When they reached the bottom, the bear rose onto its hind legs. They froze. But it only descended to where they had been on the knoll and began sniffing the ground. It wasn't looking at them, so they inched into the alders. Once they couldn't see the bear, and hoping it couldn't see them, they broke into a run.

It was 3:30 P.M. They had been pinned for an hour and a half. Karen and Marv finally arrived at the destroyed camp and realized just who had been chasing whom. They met the group, and all six hiked the remaining half mile, fully expecting the bear to pop out of every alder patch along the way. By 4:15, without incident, they found the boat.

Charles and Karen paddled the dingy out to the eighteen-foot *Arete* where a lodge employee, Rick, was manning the radio. Rick listened to Charles's story and made it clear that he felt they had been "typical dumb tourists" who had "irritated the bear into chasing them." He did, however, feel it his duty to report their experience to head ranger Charles Janda back at park headquarters thirty-five miles away in Bartlett Cove.

Communications were extremely inefficient. Messages to or from Bartlett Cove had to be relayed to the boats through a ranger outpost at Goose Bay. Two-man search crews from the Coast Guard boats, the *Arete* and the *Bossman,* carried CB radios and checked in every thirty minutes. With long amateur radio experience, Charles ended up handling some of the communications.

When Janda received Charles's relayed message, he took it seriously, wisely recognizing the danger in this new dimension of the search for Alan Precup. He promptly passed the order for men on the ground to return to the boats. All of them were unarmed. Responding with CBs, they scoffed at the idea of a bear even being where they had never seen one before. They grumbled that the plight of incompetent tourists was not reason enough to call off an important search. Nonetheless, they headed toward the boats.

While Charles was on the radio, in the most incredible of her mistakes, Karen paddled ashore and talked Marv into going back for her tent and gear. Not to be out-machoed by a girl, Marv borrowed Colin's ice ax for protection, and they left.

In the meantime, Ranger James Luthy was dispatched with a Coast Guard helicopter. After spotting a destroyed camp, he was lowered to the ground. It was perhaps three-quarters of a mile from the Seattle camp. He found scattered belongings, including Precup's credit cards, but Precup himself was nowhere around. Oddly, while the bear left nothing undisturbed, it had not eaten Precup's food. The pilot radioed the find and left.

Shortly after, a two-man search crew, returning to their boat via this same trail, also stumbled into Precup's camp—and into the bear that had given up on the Seattle group. They dropped their packs and ran. The bear, having a more macabre interest just then, did not give chase.

While all this was happening, Janda got word about Karen's latest and most naive disregard for the potential danger of bears.

He ordered her and Marv immediately picked up by helicopter. A picture of her rescue made it into an Alaskan newspaper without a word about the foolishness that preceded it.

Darkness was encroaching, and they were forty miles from the lodge at Gustavus, so all six were taken by boat to the summertime ranger outpost at Goose Bay. Two rangers had a large tent with an oil stove pitched on a pontoon raft. Asked why they were camped on water, they answered, "Bears," then set up a tent on shore for the campers who had been terrorized by one for four hours. The rangers returned to the safety of their pontoon.

The following morning, Luthy and two state police troopers returned to Precup's camp. His journal was found with the last entry dated September 11. Further search uncovered his scattered remains—now mostly bones, scalp, and clothes. The bear had returned to eat an arm it had buried.

A two-day inquest followed, along with what the Seattle four considered a fairly clear effort to cover thoughtless and incompetent Park Service actions. Waiting for an aerial search first was waiting too long, but as it turned out, Precup could not have been saved. His recovered diary indicated he was on a quest to experience firsthand "closeness" with nature. It also indicated contact with the bear over a day or two and implied that Precup may not have discouraged that contact.

More than two decades later, the ordeal stayed with the Seattle four. Dr. Peter Talbot overheard Lani, now his wife, telling their daughter about the most fearful experience of her life. She still believes that natural law would have made her the sacrificial lamb.

To this day, Dr. Charles Jackson is troubled by the fact that, despite better intentions, he ran past Lani. The rest of us can take heart from this. Few adults aren't living with some brain stem flight command they're ashamed they obeyed.

And for others who may encounter a determined bear, do we know what prevented attack? Yes. As Dr. Jackson has suggested, it was numbers. For whatever the reason, probably formidable appearance, there is no record of a grizzly ever attacking a group of three or more people. And as Lani said, the men kept their wits. The group did not panic, scatter, and divide their numbers.

GRIZZLY REMATCH

With his left foot nearly bitten off, Gregg Fischer could envision no humanly possible way to get him the eight miles back to camp through this rough Arctic country. But Alaska Master Guide James P. "Jake" Jacobson has an attitude: "If you think you can—or if you think you can't—you're probably right."

Alpine, Wyoming guide Gregg Fischer, fifty-five, learned how well bears plan the first time he helped a client take one. The hunter made a poorly placed shot, just wounding the bear, and then didn't care to follow an angry animal into the woods to finish the job. Gregg went in and found the bear on its hind legs behind a tree waiting for him. Fortunately, he spotted the bear at ten yards and was able to kill it with a quick head shot before it could attack.

He and his friend, Don Cribbins, were now hunting caribou north of the Arctic Circle, and this, too, is bear country. Grizzly bear country. Being a professional hunter with long experience at spotting game, he wanted to be in front with the partner or client directly behind him—especially in dense cover when the presence of bears is a possibility. And now they were going through a second stand of willows to reach the only place they had seen caribou. Gregg glanced back to check on Don who had been behind him through the first patch of trees and into the second. He wasn't there. Don had drifted about twenty-five yards upslope. Gregg almost yelled, "What the hell are you doing up there?" Instead, realizing they were about to break out of the willows, he decided it was probably okay. He was wrong. He heard *humph, humph,* and saw a bear on its hind legs about ten yards from Don, staring at him as if trying to figure out what he was.

Don looked up at the same *humph*ing sounds, saw the grizzly, and raised his rifle. Rain had fogged the 3X-to-9X power scope, and it was out of focus at this distance, but it was set on low power and he could see enough of the bear to make a fairly accurate shot. Nevertheless, he hesitated, aware that if he failed to hit the brain or spine, he'd be killed before the bear died.

Despite the fact that grizzlies often regard yelling as a challenge, Gregg shouted the instant he saw the bear, "Don, look out. There's a bear right smack in front of you!"

Before the words were out of his mouth, the bear dropped to all fours, and came crashing through the willows, straight at him. Gregg's safety was off when the bear came into view at ten yards, but there wasn't time to shoulder the rifle. He fired from the hip, and the bear never flinched. The grizzly looked up as it ran, fixed his eyes on him, and then dropped its head again as if he knew exactly what he had to do. Amazingly, Gregg worked the bolt of his Winchester Model 70 fast enough to chamber another .30-06 in time to fire again at five yards. He was in the act of chambering the third cartridge when the grizzly hit him, knocking him to the ground. Still gripping the rifle, Gregg pulled the trigger. Nothing happened. The empty had ejected, but the live cartridge stayed in the clip.

He was now on his stomach, trying to protect the back of his head and neck with his arms, when the bear grabbed his lower left leg. As the powerful jaws came together, the bear's head twisted sharply in a move intended to snap and crush bones. Gregg cried out in pain, and the bear bit into his left thigh, picked him up and shook, slicing flesh down to the bone from the hip nearly around to the groin, narrowly missing the leg artery. His lower leg hurt so bad that for the moment Gregg didn't even realize the bear had done serious damage to his thigh. In seconds, the attack seemed over. He could hear the grizzly leaving through the willows.

But an instant later, it didn't sound over. The bear was *humphing* again.

Certain that the bear would be right back, Gregg tried to get to his feet and reload his rifle. He pushed up with his arms and right leg, but when he tried to place weight on his left foot, the pain was so intense that he collapsed to the ground again. His hip boots prevented him from seeing the extent of damage, but the thought went through his mind when he placed weight on the foot that it had shifted as if it had detached and were no longer his foot.

"Don," he shouted, "I've been hit by a bear down here. I'm hurt pretty bad. I need you to get down here."

Don was on his way. He had seen the whole attack. It lasted less than a minute, and there had never been an opportunity to shoot at the bear without fear of hitting Gregg, too. When the bear left Gregg, however, Don did try an offhand running shot that produced no visible effect on the grizzly, except perhaps, to keep the bear in a leaving mode.

The bear had bitten through Gregg's hip boot just above the ankle, and it was evident that both leg bones were broken. It made no sense to either man, however, to waste time examining the extent of the damage. Gregg wanted out of those willows and onto the meadow where he could see the grizzly coming.

Don tried to drag him, but Gregg is an inch over six feet tall, weighs nearly 200 pounds, and Don is a slight 140-pounder. Their progress was too slow, so Gregg began pulling himself hand over hand as fast as he could go. At times, he stabbed his knife into the ground to have something to grip and pull against. The foot came flopping along behind, painfully twisting in a different direction with every stick or clump of grass it met. After pulling himself a hundred yards, he was on a flat area about three hundred yards from the river and out on a grassy meadow with a little knoll to lie on and watch for the bear. He hoped the bear would approach from the front or come in on his left side. He could use his right leg to rotate his body to the left. Doing the opposite with his left leg would be impossible.

The two men were four air miles from the lodge, but with all the ups, downs, twists, and turns, it was eight ground miles. Sixty-five-year-old Don would need to walk those eight miles as quickly as he could, carry his rifle in case he encountered a bear, take his pack because he might need emergency supplies along the way, and then lead help back to Gregg in a speedy fashion. Fear that Gregg would go into shock and die of hypothermia gave him precisely the motivation he needed.

Tripod legs for a spotting scope were in Gregg's pack, as was a rope he always carried to drag something or other. He spaced the legs one on top and one on each side of his ankle as best he could and bound them with the rope, recoiling in torment every time the foot moved.

He lay on the knoll reconsidering his often stated wish that when he has to die, he hopes it happens in Alaska. He could envision multiple ways of it happening. "If I'm not eaten by the bear, I'll bleed to death." "If something happens to Don, they may never find me." "I'll go into shock before morning, and the cold will get me." "They can't get a plane down here, and no vehicle at the lodge can cross the river." "The bear could be watching . . ."

The wind blew; the clouds spit snow. He heard rustlings. "Animals. It has to be animals." They were 155 miles above the Arctic Circle. This was all animal country, no villages, no humans, no roads for three hundred miles, no paths, only caribou and bear trails. Even if searchers found him alive, he could envision no humanly possible way to get him out in his helpless condition.

September 6, 2000, had begun as the first day without rain in a week. Lots of glassing for game had been done in the previous three days, but no serious hunting. Only Gregg and Don had spotted a small band of perhaps thirteen caribou. That morning, the two men crossed the river called Trail Creek and headed downstream toward the four miles of willow thickets near which they had seen the animals. Alaska Master Guide and owner of Arctic Rivers Guide Service, James P. "Jake" Jacobson, left the lodge with Dick May from Hawaii who wanted a bear. They stayed on the lodge side of the river and were glassing with binoculars and spotting scopes from a high knoll. Jason Moe, grandnephew of Gene Moe (see "Lethal Punch"), had pulled a muscle and intended to stay in camp, but Jake's sister, Pat, also a guide, spotted a grizzly. Jason glassed the blond bear with black feet from an upstairs window of the lodge and decided to go. Lon Palmer from Washington went along with Pat and Jason to watch the bear hunt and perhaps get a chance at caribou. Jason, who has taken elk at six hundred yards with one shot, missed the bear twice at three hundred yards. Apparently, three days of being in the rain had changed his gun's barrel bedding by swelling the wooden stock.

While glassing with 10X binoculars, Jake saw Gregg and Don enter a large willow thicket about three miles from the lodge. He went back to watching Jason's stalk when, suddenly, a sow and a three-year-old cub bolted out from the willows at a place closer to camp than where Gregg and Don had gone in. Both light-colored bears ran like they had seen the devil bear himself—and perhaps they had. The leading cause of death among grizzly bears is another grizzly. This sow may have lost a cub to an aggressive boar before. By running at breakneck speeds, then resting only by slowing down for a time, the bears went from thirteen hundred feet at the valley floor to over forty-four hundred feet at the top of a very rough mountain. They did over three thousand feet in twenty minutes, scattering sheep as they fled. Jake told Dick that he hadn't seen bears spooked that badly in the entire thirty-five years he has been guiding in this part of the Brooks Range.

Around 5:00 P.M. Jake saw a man heading back to the lodge at a very fast pace. "I have a morbid feeling about this," he said to Dick. "Something's wrong. Don might have had a heart attack." Expecting to meet Gregg at the river, he found Don instead.

"It's bad out there," Don said. "I'm afraid Gregg is going into shock."

While swiftly returning to the lodge for emergency supplies, Don recounted the attack by a huge, dark, almost black grizzly that apparently broke Gregg's left leg just above the ankle. Jake gathered up suture materials—bandages, aspirin, Tylenol, Aperine with codeine, a canteen and water, lots of candy, duct tape, his pistol, and his miter box and a piece of one-by-four wood that might combine to make a splint. Jake had spent a year working in the Marine Hospital in Baltimore in preparation for being sent to Vietnam. After that, he came to Alaska to fly from village to village providing emergency dental care to the natives, so his medical knowledge was considerable. That lasted twenty years before guiding became more attractive.

"Dick, you wait here until Pat gets back with Lon and Jason," he said. "Then get down to where Gregg is. It's going to take all of us to get him out. But I don't want a bunch of rifles there. We'll have enough to carry."

Like the two light-colored bears going up the mountain, Jake made time by alternating fifty paces of running with fifty paces of walking. Don, despite his age and his having made this trip twice that day, was only about a hundred and twenty yards behind when Jake arrived at the willows.

The rain-soaked ground was cold for Gregg to lie on, and pulling himself across the wet meadow to the mound to begin his long wait had only compounded the problem. He had been shaking for four hours. By 7:00 P.M., darkness was beginning to close in when unmistakably he heard a noise somewhere behind him. He couldn't raise himself to turn and look, but Gregg felt certain it had to be the bear.

Meanwhile, Jake had fired his pistol and hearing no response, feared Gregg had passed out. And maybe he had, because now Jake fired two more times, and Gregg lifted his head in surprise to see Jake's white beard and cap above willows up on the hill. Jake, not the bear, had passed behind Gregg and was about to enter the thicket where the bear had gone.

"Here!" Gregg managed to yell. "I'm down here."

Back at the lodge, after hearing Dick's story, everybody went into action, gathering things to take to the attack site. "Before we leave too quickly," Pat suggested, "lets all take an extra few minutes and try to think of anything imaginable we might need."

Pat thought of shock and made thermoses of hot bouillon broth. Fortunately, plenty of extra flashlight batteries went along as well as codeine, aspirin, and candy bars. Pat and the men at the lodge managed to join the others by 9:00 P.M.

Jake already had the splint on Gregg's ankle. He could see enough to know that the foot was only hanging on by parts of the skin and flesh that hadn't been cut by teeth. The torn boot was helping hold things together, so that was left undisturbed. The board had to be cut to length, but the miter box fit nicely over the ankle. Rope and duct tape held the splint together. Jake stood Gregg on his right leg, hoping that with the splint's support he might be able to walk. Gregg tried to put weight on his left foot, but the pain was intolerable.

After four hours of believing that there was no way out of this, and now finding that the splint didn't help him stand, either, Gregg's anxiety soared. "Don't worry," reassured Jake in his calm, self-confident voice. "I'll get you out of here no matter what." Jake dragged him for about three hundred yards before the others arrived, but it was obvious that a better way was needed.

Lon remembers that the initial idea for moving Gregg was to use the old army or fireman's carry—"grab a victim's arm over one shoulder, a same-side leg over the other, and carry the victim with his stomach against your back. His body is perpendicular to yours." It was quickly recognized that this is workable where balance can be maintained, but impossible where boots already sink over the ankles without Gregg's two hundred pounds. And falling with Gregg would be inevitable stumbling through knee- to waist-high dwarf birch.

Gregg thought that if he put an arm around the shoulders of Jake and Jason, he could hop along between them. That routine lasted a quarter mile at most. Progress was too slow and painful. (They would later discover the bones had been crushed into shards, and each movement of his leg jabbed pointed fragments into the flesh inside it.)

When Pat had the men thinking about taking everything they could imagine as useful, somebody grabbed an eight-by-ten green canvas tarp, believing that it might make a travois. Lon cut willow poles and rolled the tarp edges around them, then secured everything with duct tape, forming more of a litter than a travois. Unfortunately, the biggest willows above the Arctic Circle are about eight feet tall and maybe an inch and a half in diameter—and these were green and springy. When Gregg was placed on the makeshift travois, it collapsed.

"Okay—if a travois leaves Gregg dragging along on the ground," Jake reasoned, "why not at least try a drag that's easier to pull? Or push." This time they rolled one end of the tarp around a horizontal pole and secured it with tape. The ends of the pole stuck out far enough on each side that two men could stand behind them, hold the ends against their stomachs, push forward against the poles, and drag Gregg along behind them on the tarp. Gregg slid off, so now he was moved higher on the tarp with both arms hooked over the pole at the elbows.

Pat went on ahead about thirty yards to scout for caribou trails or other places with fewer obstacles. Don walked between Pat and the men, shining his flashlight back as a beacon to follow or sometimes staying closer, using his light to show them where to place their feet when obstacles became a problem. The "horses," as they called those who pushed, or sometimes pulled on the "singletree," tried to make as many of twenty-five steps as possible before pausing to rest. If one tired, another relieved him. When Gregg's arms and shoulders became too sore to keep them hooked over the pole, two men took new positions as horses and the other two held onto Gregg's arms to keep him from sliding off.

Except for Gregg's foot bouncing along in constant pain, this worked fairly well until they needed to cross a creek. There would be six of those before they'd come to the river. This country is a broad valley with Trail Creek running through it and drainage from the mountains on both sides flowing into the river through these side-creek tributaries. Unfortunately, Gregg and Don had found the only caribou on the west side of the river. The east side goes up from that low brushy area to somewhat higher ground that has good caribou trails and much easier walking. The west side has the dwarf birch that tangles around the shins, as well as lots of boggy muskeg producing precariously unstable footing. Crossing the river would have saved them half the travel time and immeasurable pain, but the rains had made that impossible.

Wading the creeks required Gregg to again try to hop along between two men, usually Lon and Jason who were the largest. All this bouncing jolted Gregg's foot, causing him excruciating pain, so the men soon came up with a new "carry," requiring a third man to walk in front and hold the right leg up while the left dangled. Sometimes, a fourth man held up the left leg as well by gripping underneath the leg and above the knee.

The worst obstacles were the boggy muskegs with tussocks growing every couple of feet. These bowling ball–sized, mushroom-shaped tufts of grasses (sedge bunches with many stems) are deceiving. They are bound together by plant roots. They give the appearance of solid footing, but stepping on them is likely to result in a sprained ankle. Freezing and thawing push up hummocks or small hillocks with bowls in between, producing a slowness of movement on the uneven, mucky terrain.

Dragging Gregg through boggy conditions was making him much too wet; so two men lifted the canvas by the pole ends. Two others grabbed the trailing corners of the opposite end of the canvas, creating a sort of canvas "basket" in which to carry him. The four-man hold kept most of him out of the water most of the time, especially if the men could march in step.

By midnight, the four carriers felt as if their arms were pulling out of their sockets. Everybody looked for what rarely existed—dry places in a bog where they could put Gregg down and rest. Jake, the dentist and lodge owner, had been giving Gregg aspirin and codeine for pain, and stuffing him with candy to maintain a sugar level that might ward off shock. "Okay," Jake, the ex-marine, snapped about 2:00 A.M. "Put him down. We'll take a twenty-minute rest." Five minutes later he shouted, "Time's up. Let's go. I don't want him getting any chillier than he already is."

Everybody would return to lifting and pulling, feeling that they couldn't possibly do this all the way back to the lodge—but knowing that they would. Gregg slid off the tarp at least a hundred times, he was wet and cold, and he knew how sore the carriers were. Around 2:00 A.M. he became despondent. "Hey, guys," he said, "this is never going to work. Just shoot me." Jake shot back, "We're going home tonight. And, you're coming with us."

Pat's eyes still fill with tears when she remembers Gregg sometimes moaning in pain or even yelping when his foot caught on something, and then seconds later apologizing "for putting you guys through so much." As the night wore on, Pat sensed when he should have warm liquid. Jake plied him with candy bars until Gregg didn't want to see another and began hiding them. He kept asking to rest (which is what people in trauma want, but go into shock if they get too much of). Jake's rest periods continued to be short.

Jason noticed that Gregg's jacket had become so soaked that water could be wrung from it. Around 3:00 A.M. temperatures had fallen below freezing, so Jason removed his own Gore-Tex and Thinsulate hunting coat and put it on Gregg. At times, the strong coat was used as a drag.

One young bull moose stood and watched in apparent amazement as they labored past.

Finally, just before daybreak, the exhausted crew arrived at Trail Creek which they'd have to cross to reach Jake's lodge. The last obstacle was an intimidating, high cutbank. It would be a steep hundred-foot slide on gravel, shale, and exposed larger rock. Gregg took one look and said, "Oh, no!"

But he went. Jake and Jason scooted him down, one on each side on their rumps, so he wouldn't slip and roll. Lon went down ahead to be ready to help in case anybody did slip. In minutes, they were at the bottom starting a three-man carry across three channels with four feet of water.

Jake's lodge is in a willow flat along the stream, and below that is a long gravel bar with low willows where he had cleared enough trees to land his Piper Super Cub. A couple hundred yards beyond was the southern edge of the bar where they had taken two three-wheelers the evening before. Jake had a small utility trailer hitched to one of the three-wheelers, so they promptly hauled Gregg to the lodge.

Dawn was just beginning to break, about 7:30 A.M., and everyone had been up since 6:00 the morning before. Jake knew he was fatigued, too, so he didn't dare try to fly the 140 miles to Kotzebue. He lit the oil heater, dressed Gregg's wounds, resplinted him, and then placed him beside the heater in two sleeping bags. He was rather blue, and his temperature was down to a dangerous ninety-three degrees. Everybody sacked in except Pat, who monitored Gregg's temperature and roused Jake when it seemed normal three hours later.

With the backseat out of the plane, Gregg could lie on sleeping bags during the ninety-minute flight to Kotzebue. The doctor at the hospital took one look at Gregg's wounds, exclaimed, "Oh, my God," almost pitched her cookies, and asked Jake to scrub up and help her. She thought the thigh was infected, but Jake's year of patching people together before surgery in Baltimore had taught him that she was looking at a little area of fat.

X-rays showed that both leg bones were more than simply broken. They were crushed into shards. After four hours in the emergency room, it was clear that a specialist at a larger hospital would have to set the leg. The doctor called for a medivac.

Jake had been told that jet medivac flights cost around $50,000. Gregg, who was then still unconscious, didn't have medical insurance or that kind of money. "Anyhow," Jake said, "after what Gregg endured the night before, a seat on a commercial jet would be duck soup for him. Furthermore, the X-rays had shown staples and stainless steel wire already in his leg, meaning he already had an orthopedic surgeon back in Wyoming." Jake cancelled the medivac flight, as well as plans to send him to an Anchorage hospital.

Jake's hands had been on Gregg in one way or another since finding him on that little knoll, and now he continued his care by proxy. At Jake's request, his son-in-law accompanied Gregg to Anchorage, and retired guide Jim Cann met them and arranged Gregg's connecting flight to Wyoming.

At the airport, Alaska Airlines upgraded Gregg to first class without charge. Back in the Lower Forty-eight, one shuttle was a small plane that had no mechanism to hoist Gregg aboard. He sat down on the concrete runway, and then backed himself up the steps one at a time. His girlfriend met him at Jackson and drove him to the doctor. The doctor was dismissive at first. "I can't see you right now. I have to be at a volleyball game," he said. And then he saw the wounds. His next "right now" was preceded with "operating room."

Gregg fully expected to be patched up and back for a rematch with that grizzly when the next season opened September 1, 2001. Jake applied for his permit, but the drawing was over-subscribed by eight and Gregg came in last. It was just as well because the bone didn't mend after the first operation. In fact, the pain was so intense that he considered amputation.

Jake applied again in 2002. This time the over-subscription was just one . . . Gregg Fischer. Two operations later, the bone had mended and the pain was gone. Because of missing pieces, however, his foot points nine degrees off straight forward. It would require perhaps several breaks, turns, and regrowths in the bones above the ankle. Not surprisingly, Gregg refused—as he did the medivac, as he did the hospital stay after the first operation ("You let me go home, or you'll soon find me gone."), and as he did the $2,500 rabies shot a doctor ordered without his knowledge ("I had a friend in Alaska check around the state, and he found only three cases of rabies in bears—ever."). Gregg's attitude was: "I'll take my chances."

The doctor swore at him over that one.

Gregg was successful in the drawing for 2003. "I will recognize that bear," Gregg said before heading back to Alaska. "Don and I saw that grizzly three times during six days before the attack. He was behaving crazy then. We watched him acting up all the way across the big mountain ridge. He'd prance around and jump up and down like he was angry or agitated. Once he looked as if he were stomping grapes. Then he loped off to the river. A big, dark, silvertip boar. I've hunted bears for thirty years, and I've never seen one act as berserk as this bear.

"I'll know him when I see him."

Jake's grandsons, Spencer and Stuart, while unloading supplies from the plane on August 24, had seen a blondish grizzly swatting runway markers eleven hundred feet away. Suddenly, the bear rose up onto its hind legs, saw them, and charged. Spencer fired a shot in front of the running bear, causing it to pause. A second warning shot drove it into the willows. Later, in a knee-high brushy area forty to eighty yards from the lodge, scats, bits of meat-hanging line, bones, and other scattered remains clearly indicated that a grizzly was spending entirely too much time near camp for safety.

On September 1, Gregg and Jake left camp to hunt upcreek and found a big bull caribou in a band of twenty-five just a quarter mile from the lodge. Gregg took the bull, which turned out to be the best of the season at Jake's camp. But during the night of September 4, a grizzly made off with two caribou quarters and left a big footprint near the meat rack, exacerbating an already tense situation.

The next morning, a blondish bear entered a willow patch on the southeast side of Trail Creek. Despite the blustery cold, Gregg and Jake took turns watching for it until 5:00 P.M. when they headed back to finish cooking a turkey dinner. On the way, they intercepted a blond boar, also on its way to the camp.

Gregg's attacker had been a dark boar, so he knew this wasn't the one he'd sworn to kill. But the temptation was irresistible. This was a "Toklat" grizzly. (Toklat River translates to "dishwater river," so using the term for a bear suggests a dishwater blond.) It was creamy white with chocolate legs and a dark stripe down its back. Even the groin was well furred. Having a taxidermist's eye for rare beauty in a pelt, Gregg couldn't resist. That cost him his bear permit, but it was his birthday, and what a gift this was. Both men also figured that the dangerous camp bear was now history.

Wrong. The next day the camp awoke to find the A-frame meat rack demolished, dragged five yards south, and every piece of meat either chewed on or eaten. There was no other place to hang additional meat, so Jake rebuilt the rack. This time, however, he added a trip line to a bell to warn clients of the bear's presence. It is legal in Alaska to dispatch bears that are threatening life or property, so he also loaded a shotgun with buckshot and slugs for nighttime protection by patrons of the outhouse. No bear raided camp during the night.

On September 7, everyone retired at 10:30 P.M., and about twenty minutes later Bob Johnson, the only other hunter with a bear permit, heard the bell ring. He quietly got into position, fired, and the bear charged off into the darkness. Bob was confident that his shot was well placed, but nobody considered it prudent to search for a possibly wounded grizzly at night. By first light it could be seen behind a willow about twenty feet from where it had been shot. Lying dead on the ground, the grizzly looked very dark. Jake thought it would have appeared more grizzled in life—provided conditions were dry. Under the very wet conditions of 2000, however, this big boar would have looked as dark as Gregg had described his attacker. And Gregg did believe it was a boar.

Later, as they posed the bear for pictures, Jake discovered that the front leg had not been used normally for some time. Marks were on the backs of the claws from being dragged along. Also apparent was an old injury to the right hip.

"Well, Jake," Gregg pointed out, "You'll remember that I said my first shot at that charging bear in the 2000 season had been a bit high. That explains the hip wound. I thought the second shot at point blank range went into the chest, but apparently it hit the leg instead. I'm positive this is the boar that attacked me three years ago."

With this much evidence matching Gregg's account of the attack, Jake, too, believes that there are no rounds left in the grizzly rematch.

LETHAL PUNCH

Gene Moe stood tall and tried to appear menacing as he dragged his battered body toward this bear that was coming at him for the fifth time. He would not allow her the added confidence of thinking the fight had gone out of him.

Gene Moe snapped his head around at the ferociously loud and deep bawling roar of a close and angry bear. At first glimpse, he knew he was in for the fight of his life. This was no trotting charge of a bluffing bear. Both front paws reached forward together in each leap of a galloping bear going in for the kill. Gene made one instinctive step toward his rifle, just five feet away, and then recognized the futility of dropping an inferior weapon to grab a superior one he'd never have time to shoot. The knife he had been using to skin a Sitka blacktail deer was still in his hand, so he thrust it forward to meet the raging bear's wide-open mouth, hoping to shove it down her throat. He was keenly aware that he could lose a hand, or more, but no better defense presented itself.

Gene might not have been in this life-threatening predicament had his partner of the day been able to follow their plan. Two years earlier, the same partner and Gene had just skinned out the hindquarters of a deer when a Kodiak bear appeared and plopped down a hundred yards away, probably called by the dinner bell shot. "Hey, we've got company," Gene said. "Get the two quarters onto my backboard, and let's get out of here." They were a meager fifty yards away when the bear arrived to carry off the rest of the deer.

This year, they were camped on Afognak Island northwest of the village of Kodiak, but Gene, sixty-nine, and his son, Karl, forty-four, and the two partners, Tom Frohlick, forty-four, and Steve Fitzpatrick, forty-eight, both employees of Gene's concrete contracting business, motored their skiff across the straits and down about ten miles to the lower end of Raspberry Island to hunt Sitka blacktails. Gene's plan was to position Steve on a ridge, move out about two hundred yards, and circle to move a deer toward him. If by late in the day, Steve hadn't gotten a deer, and Gene got a chance for a buck, he would take it. The rules called for the partner to be alert for the shot, and then listen for the owl hoot. Because it doesn't disturb deer or other nearby wildlife, these hunters use the hoot to signal that their deer is down. It would then be the partner's job to join Gene and watch his back during the field dressing. About that time Steve dropped his cap's earflaps.

"Can you hear with those flaps down?" Gene asked.

"Oh yeah," Steve answered, but later he heard neither shot nor hoot. And the bear bearing down on Gene wanted and needed more than a gut pile. This was November 1, 1999. The berry crop had been poor, a severe previous winter had killed an estimated third of the deer, and Asian ships with twenty-mile nets were making clear-cuts in the ocean's fishery. Few Pacific salmon came upstream at Raspberry Island to spawn, die, and provide the fat-building nutrition essential for bears to hibernate.

Raspberry has an open grassy top, but at lower elevations moss hangs from big timber in the world's northernmost rainforest. That year, snows had driven the deer down to the forest. Gene did watch a beautiful buck for twenty minutes, but it spooked before his partner could get a shot. About two o'clock, he saw another buck and decided to take it while there was still enough daylight to get it back to Afognak. Steve didn't show up, so he began skinning it out alone. All the meat was off the carcass and laid out on plastic, and the heart and liver were in his hands when he heard the bloodcurdling roar. His only chance of survival depended on what he could do quickly with the four-inch blade on his Model 110 Buck folding knife. And that chance was rapidly diminishing. Foam does bubble forth profusely from the mouths of excited bears, and this hungry sow was so excited that Gene now saw more foam than head. He could only aim his blade at the center and hope.

The knife slid alongside her head, and the bear bit Gene's right arm above the elbow, taking out a big chunk of flesh. He could feel her trying to tear the arm off completely. He quickly reached over her head with his left hand to jab a finger in her eye, but came to an ear first and rammed his finger in as hard and far as it would go, then twisted. This experience proved to be so new and so intolerable that she relaxed her grip on his arm and tried to pull away, but Gene's left arm was over her neck. Thinking he might put her on the ground in a more helpless position, he attempted to bulldog her as he had young bulls during his youth on the farm in Minnesota. Big mistake. She flipped her neck and threw him eight feet.

Having watched bears doing lots of berry picking and digging, Gene knew she'd swing at him with her right paw. Like humans, the vast majority of bears are right-handed. This one stood up on her hind legs, arms outstretched in scarecrow fashion, and began circling, picking her moment to end this confrontation. A grizzly can decapitate a cow with one swipe; a Kodiak brown is even bigger, and Gene knew his head would come off a lot easier than a cow's. He was also certain that she was standing on her hind legs to place that right paw at the best level to accomplish this. He tried to move closer to his rifle while focusing his eyes on nothing but that right paw. He saw it coming the instant it started. And at that same instant, he jerked his head back the way a boxer dodges a right hook. She missed, but came close enough that one claw split his ear and almost tore off the ear lobe.

Since that failed, she dropped to all fours, hit his legs, and knocked him on his back. She'd be on top of him next, bouncing or biting to crush his ribs or skull, so he jerked both heavily booted feet together and kicked upward with all his strength as she came flying in. The collision knocked her off to the side, and Gene leaped to his feet.

She began circling him again, and like a prizefighter up against a taller man with a longer reach, Gene knew that he had to get inside that right paw to survive. She was beating him to death. She came at him fast on all fours, and this time Gene was stepping off with his left foot, right foot still on the ground, as the paw started to swing. The paw missed and swung around his back, so she bit a large chunk out of his right leg above the knee instead. The pain was severe, but now Gene was inside the right front paw and against the bear's shoulder with his left arm over her neck. His right arm had no feeling, and flesh from above the elbow hung down to his fingers, yet the knife remained locked in his grip. He reached over the neck and stabbed four times as hard as he could. Then changing tactics, he moved closer to the jaw to slice the neck so he could push his knife and fist into the cut to stab deeper.

The sow tried to stop Gene by raising him off the ground with her right paw. He hung on and kept cutting the hole deeper, but he couldn't hold her when she dropped him to push away with both front feet. Nevertheless, before her head pulled out from under his left arm, he managed one more hard stab into the deep slash near her jaw. Blood squirted all over them both. Immediately, this Kodiak brown wanted a breather between rounds and circled out beyond the little arena of beaten-down snow where they'd been fighting.

Noticing that some of the fight was going out of her, Gene yelled, "Bear, the Lord's on my side, so come on!"

She did. And as she ran, Moe could see blood still gushing from the cut nearest the jaw. He also noticed that her head was cocked oddly sideways, suggesting that the last stab had probably gone deep enough to injure a vertebra. Terribly battered with loose skin and flesh hanging from his arm, claw gashes in his shoulders, and painfully dragging his right leg, six-foot three-inch Gene tried to stand tall and move toward her looking as menacing as possible. He would not allow her the added confidence of thinking the fight had gone out of him.

Whatever she thought, it did not stop her from charging—though not with the speed demonstrated earlier.

All Gene had left now was a little prayer and the advice of a dog-musher friend who said a blow to the nose from a light club he carried would stop nearly any animal, even kill some. Gene drew back his left fist, and as the bear leaped at him, he threw the hardest punch of his life. He missed the nose, but struck her cocked head just under the eye. The impact of the punch combined with the momentum of the 750-pound brown was so powerful that his arm and hand went white and he had no feeling left in the knuckles. The sow's head twitched, and she bared two front teeth that were still covered with Gene's "meat," as he tells it, before suddenly dropping with her paws under her body. Her cocked head straightened with the blow, and her nose pulled downward during her fall, ramming it into the moss. She lay motionless.

Gene had seen so many animals go down that he knew it's a brain or spine shot when one drops with its feet under it. Hit other organs, it will go down with its feet or legs out from under its body. He believed this one was dead from damage he had inflicted to the spine with his knife and fist. But he wasn't taking any chances; he stepped back to get his rifle. He did not want this bear to unexpectedly revive and attack him one more time. Before he could shoot, however, he had to first free his hand of the knife—but found he couldn't relax his grip. Eventually, he was able to pull his fingers from the knife with his teeth, but then the loose skin and flesh from his arm fell over the scope of his rifle. Finally, he managed to raise the rifle high enough to get the flesh off to the side, and then lower it to shoot the bear twice in the chest.

A little fur flew both times, but the bear never twitched. Clearly, Gene's lethal punch had finished breaking the vertebra of his 750-pound opponent. Gene's ordeal, however, was far from over. He was two miles from the boat, feeling dizzy from loss of blood, and still bleeding badly. He pulled the hanging flesh back up on his right arm and wrapped a plastic bag around it as best he could. His hunting pants—purchased in 1948, made of quarter-inch thick wool, and worn only for the annual hunts—had probably reduced the potential damage when the bear bit a chunk out of his right leg. At least for now, he could still move on his feet. He had not seen the cubs, which later evidence showed the sow had, but as a precaution, he picked up his rifle as he left. He could easily meet other bears on Raspberry Island. They have excellent noses, and he would smell like easy pickings—a bloody, wounded, and half-dead prey animal.

He doesn't know how far he got before exhaustion forced him to lie down in the snow. He ate some and rested. When he felt it was time to move on, however, he couldn't sit up. Finally, he struggled onto his stomach and pushed himself off the ground with his left arm and leg. At this point, he recognized what carrying extra weight was doing to the limits of his strength. Meeting another bear now seemed less of a gamble than whether he'd reach the beach at all. He abandoned his rifle.

At least twice he had to again lie down in the snow to rest. During one of those rests he remembers trying to die. "Lord, take me home," he begged, but it wasn't his time. So Gene struggled on, sometimes walking, sometimes crawling.

At one point, it appeared as if he was about to lose in the gamble of discarding his rifle—and his death wish would soon be fulfilled. He was hearing sounds from an animal too big to be anything but another bear. Yet being eaten alive did not exactly seem like a reasonable answer to prayer, so Gene remained motionless long after the noises ceased. If it had been a bear, wind direction had played in his favor.

Struggling through alder thickets was the most difficult challenge of the entire two-mile trek. The tree limbs would snag the plastic bag and yank it off his right arm. He'd stop, pull the hanging flesh back up and rewrap it, only to have it happen over and over again.

Finally, Gene spotted an opening in the woods and knew he was right on target. Within two hundred yards of the beach, he could go no farther. He wearily halted, yelling for help, hoping somebody was near the boat. He was fortunate. Tom and Steve were already there and responded immediately, warming him with another coat and a full-length flotation vest. Steve had not heard the last two shots, either.

It was the custom among these hunters that the first to get back to the boat around 4:00 P.M. would fire his rifle as a signal that it was time to come in. The others would return answering shots, and everybody would be out of the woods before dark. They fired the routine shot and Karl Moe answered, but then Tom and Steve began calling excitedly, trying to hurry him in so they could get Gene to medical help more quickly. Unfortunately, Karl could not understand their words and concluded that a shot followed by loud, excited voices meant that a bear was somewhere in between him and them. He was packing out venison and certainly not wanting a bear to catch the scent. Instead of hurrying him in, the calls slowed Karl into greater caution, but he speeded up when he got close enough to understand. He was thoroughly shocked by his father's appearance. The three quickly got Gene into the skiff and headed for the nearest habitation: the Silver Salmon Lodge owned by Peter and Barabel Guttchen.

Peter saw the skiff motoring into the bay with men waving wildly. As he walked down to ask what was wrong, he was astonished to see a man chewed and torn beyond belief step out of the boat and walk up the beach toward the lodge. A new front room was being built on the beach side of the lodge, so Gene also walked around to a door in the rear, refusing to be carried. He lay on the living room floor while Tom carefully rearranged the flesh on his right arm and bound it with an Ace bandage provided by Barabel. Karl wrapped his dad's right leg with strips torn from her apron.

The Guttchens had the only radio-telephone in the vicinity, and immediately called the Coast Guard at Kodiak. By luck, they were going on maneuvers and had a helicopter already ten feet off the ground. With the normal preparation time of forty-five minutes eliminated, they quickly arrived at the lodge. By that time, the bandaging was finished and Gene was in a sleeping bag. One look at him convinced the crew to forgo further emergency treatment and get him to the hospital as quickly as possible. But getting him out of the narrow door on a stretcher posed a problem—which the resourceful Peter promptly solved. The siding was not yet installed on the front wall, so he grabbed his chain saw, cut out two studs, along with the plywood between, and out Gene went.

Gene was flown to the then three-year-old, twenty-three-bed hospital at the little fishing village of Kodiak, where, without a break, Dr. Barry Goldsmith spent twelve hours caring for him, seven of them stitching the wounds. Bear bites are notorious for causing serious bacterial infections, but Gene contracted none at all. Four years later, the feeling had not returned in two of the knuckles in the left hand, which punched the bear.

The day after the attack, Gene's hunting partners returned to Raspberry Island to find the rifle and knife and skin the bear. Alaska law requires that any bear taken in self-defense without a tag must be turned over to Fish and Game. Gene later bought back the hide at the annual auction. The partners found the blood trail very easy to follow—sometimes drops, sometimes a spray, some smears on branches, some on trees he had leaned against, and three pools where he lay down. Behind a log with a large smear of blood, they found the rifle. Finally, as they followed the trail back to the attack site, two young bears were standing over the few remains of Gene's deer. They were probably the dead bear's two-and-a-half-year-old cubs that she was trying to drive off so she could have another offspring that winter during hibernation.

Back in the hospital, Gene overheard two nurses discussing how he was too old to heal properly. The next day, however, the doctor was asking what medic put his arm back together so expertly. "Tom Frohlick," Gene answered, "a cement finisher who works with us." (Annually, to make his employees more aware, careful, and competent in an emergency, he has them take an eight-hour class in first aid. Gene himself certainly benefited from his employee's training.) Two other reasons he could outfight a bear? He never smoked and he worked hard all his life. The doctor would later say that Gene has the muscle tone of a thirty-year-old man.

Gene offers one more tip to those who hunt in bear country. He began a fascination with studying animals while a boy trapping with his dad and has never gotten over it. Something he has noticed many times, but never told anyone until now, is how raven behavior ties in with deer hunting in bear territory. "When a raven flies over and sees you," Gene says, "he'll give a squawk or two. If you keep watching him, you'll probably hear him squawk again and notice that he's flying over another ravine. I figured if he squawks when he sees me, he's squawking when he sees something else. When the wind has been in my face, I've sneaked over to see what's there, and sure enough, I'd find a deer in that ravine. But you have to be careful. It could be a bear with a kill or cubs to defend. About half of the time, when I'd start to get close, I'd see a bear coming from the other direction. I don't know for sure if bears are smart enough to catch on to raven behavior, but I take the possibility seriously. I've certainly had enough experience with rifle shots calling bears to dinner."

HOW TO BE SAFE IN BEAR COUNTRY

From a course once taught by Bob Brown, formerly an Alaska state trooper, this is powerful information for anyone who is—or will be—in bear country.

"Nine times out of ten, bears won't maul you if you know the rules," Brown advised. "There's a winning way, and a losing way." He documented the "losing" part with a photograph of a person stretched on the ground whose body has disappeared with the exception of head and pelvic bones, two ribs, and some clothing.

"There's more to staying alive than clear thinking," Brown said, tapping the photo. "This man was a clear thinker, but remember, bears think, too. They smell, hear, see, show off, protect their young, assert their rights, run faster, and swim better than you ever will."

What Brown pounded home is simple: "Anticipate a bear. Learn to expect one every second in the bush. Imagine a bear sitting beyond the next hill; guess what its personality may be like; picture what it may be doing."

Brown was first introduced to bears when he met a bear killer who worked for a paper company in Washington State. The man had killed five thousand bears in twenty-five years to save spruce trees that were being destroyed faster than they could be replaced by bears that would girdle the trees and claw the bark.

"In those years, there were no restrictions on bears," Brown recounted. "They were killed in lots of ways, including cyanide pellets. I saw my first Alaska bear when I moved from Washington to Kodiak, Alaska, in 1965 to work as a police officer. During the next three years, I encountered twenty unusual bears that left definite impressions on me."

"Once, I was walking up a salmon stream that was lined by steep canyon walls. Suddenly, I saw a sow and cubs catching Dolly Varden trout ahead of me in the creek, and fifty yards behind me I spotted a lone bear fishing. I didn't know which way to go, so I foolishly scrambled into thick alders on higher ground. They were so thick that I couldn't stand up, so I crawled on my hands and knees. A very bad thing to do. Finally, I straightened up and made a lot of noise so that the loner could see me because that seemed like a better idea than running into the cubs. But in any case, I was trapped. After a while, the lone bear moved upstream and forgot about me—I was lucky."

Brown based his bear lectures on a file cabinet of bear encounters he has documented in Alaska, and from talks with persons who had recovered in the hospital from being badly mauled. The following interview is based on questions Brown has been asked over the years.

Do bears have personalities?

Definitely. Their behavior, like that of children, stems in part from their "home" training and where they happen to live. Some bears are spoiled. On Admiralty Island in Alaska, bears are more aggressive. They are bold and ready for a fight. On Kodiak Island, the bears are bigger. They have a casual way of wandering up to fish-drying racks or fish wheels and helping themselves.

What do you mean by "spoiled" bear?

Like a spoiled child, a spoiled bear is most likely to stay that way. Let me give some examples. When the pipeline was being built around Valdez, Alaska, I was involved in the protection of wildlife during the construction. We had a black bear that felt very at home destroying windshields on trucks. The bear would climb onto a vehicle, take the rubber gasket in hand, and pop out the glass like a banana from its peel. The glass wouldn't even shatter. Then he would crawl into the truck and rummage for food. I also know of a sow and two yearlings that tore up ten houses. To get inside, they pulled pieces of siding off the house. In one home, part of the roof was taken off, and, in another, they ate the entire sofa except for the springs and wood. One spoiled bear had a habit of wandering into construction camps and breaking apart 12-volt batteries. Another had a love for buried phone lines. People have dug pits and used sprays and electric fences to thwart prankster bears, but often you have to remove the bear and get it far away, because it won't change. We have learned that spoiled bears learn their behavior from the sow and then later pass it on to their young.

What about relocating bears?

You can transport a nuisance bear from one place to another. There was a brown bear transplanted more than fifty miles to an uninhabited island seven miles from the mainland. The water was known for its strong tides and rough waves. A month later, the bear had found its way back to its old haunts. It is very expensive to hire an aircraft to hold a bear and carry it far enough away to prevent its return.

Does relocation ever work?

I guess so, but our results are the same as those in most national parks: the bears find a way back. There are cases in which the animal has traveled hundreds of miles to find the place it calls home.

Which areas do bears prefer?

Thick woods (especially when the salmon are running), salmon streams, and kill sites, such as one where a moose has been taken and not all of the viscera has been removed from the scene. During hunting season, if you can't carry a moose out at one time, you can expect a bear to be there when you return for the meat. Bears have powerful noses. Recently in Kodiak, hunters were complaining that the shot of a rifle signaled a bear like a dinner bell. Hunters could not even get their animals skinned before a bear had arrived at the kill and claimed the meat. Some said the bears reasoned that a gunshot meant fresh food and raced for it.

Is every bear ferocious?

Yes, though its actions may belie this. When my wife and I were building our house in Eagle River, Alaska, a brown bear came inside, helped itself to a picnic table stacked with well-covered food from the night before, and made a mess of the place. I was sleeping in an adjacent trailer when I heard my dog bark, and I got up to investigate. The bear ignored me and then stared at me through the window.

Why do bears seem tame?

A warning: I got a call from people who said that a bear had appeared in the neighborhood and had hung around like a pet dog. People began to put dog food out for it. The bear would come on porches and eat dog biscuits. People called him Joe. One day, some Audubon Society members asked me where they could observe bears, so I sent them to a dump not far from that neighborhood. Joe was there, and the group was happily taking pictures of him when a man drove up, shot the bear, put the carcass in his pickup, and drove away. The Auduboners pursued him to a bridge and threatened to throw him and his son into the water if either of them moved before we got there. The nature lovers grieved over the death of this "tame, cute bear." The man thought that he had done a good thing in ridding the neighborhood of a menace.

What is rule number one around any bear?

Avoid surprise. Give notice by screaming, yelling, singing, and pounding. Think of it like this: if you stand nose to nose with your neighbor, you will encroach on his territory. He'll get upset. Bears are no different, but their territory is multiplied. Instead of inches, we are talking about yards. Each bear feels protective of its respective area from fifty to one hundred yards, and if you get inside it, you have encroached and he'll let you know it.

But how can people keep from encroaching?

Watch the bear. If you have moved into its turf and it sees you, the bear will go through a series of gyrations. It will walk back and forth in front of you, showing its body broadside. It is strutting its stuff, giving you an opportunity to retreat. The bear may urinate and scratch the ground as another way of letting you know that this is its area. One man saw a bear jump around like a rabbit, the hairs on the back of its neck standing straight up, and he thought that the bear had flipped. He got close and took some pictures. In the process, the bear knocked him down and mauled him.

What about a bear's sense of timing?

Timing is different in bear country. You can't always vacate on a dime. You have to remember this: you travel on human time, and the bear travels on bear time. Bears move like army tanks through underbrush so thick that a human could hardly crawl through it. Bears can part the weeds while moving at thirty miles an hour, snapping trees and stomping out their own trails as they go.

How do you analyze a bear?

The same way you would analyze a person. Some people will flip out, become temporarily insane, do strange things. You can insist that the majority of bears behave in a particular way, but then you find one that is different and right away people want a photo of it. Well, forget the photos. Watch what the bear is doing, but always make sure that you have an escape route. We tell hikers to take to the water, if nothing else, because most bears will remain on shore and watch. Remember, though, that bears are powerful swimmers. The number of times they have chased humans in the water in Alaska is rare—but try not to be an exception.

Are people ever safe in the water?

Probably not. But you can learn a lot about your favorite species of bear by watching it in the water. Bears can dive. On the McNeil River in Alaska, the bears are so well known for their individual water antics that each has been named. Bears also have different ways of fishing. I have watched bears chase fish up onto a beach. I have seen them swat at fish and claw them up out of the water. I have seen a hungry bear show tremendous persistence and patience. Each bear has its own fishing hole. A lesser bear will leave a big bear strictly alone and stay out of its fishing spot. In many ways, bears' actions remind me of human behavior. A loud, powerful bear will show its strength like a man flexing his muscles on the beach. The bear will prance back and forth, as though to say. "I am bigger than you. Stay clear."

Do you discourage people from hiking?

No. I encourage them. Bears are remarkable creatures, and hikers are very likely to see them. About 95 percent of all encounters are brief. You'll catch a glimpse of a bear's rear end, or see his footprints or his debris. But you must remember the rules.

Which rules?

Before you set foot in bear country, learn which type of bear you may be running into and how you should respond to it. Certain behaviors will provoke an attack, and certain things will prevent one. If you are near cubs, you are a threat, and a sow is going to do all she can to get you out of there. With black bears, you are less likely to be attacked, though, because the sow has trained her cubs to take to a tree when danger threatens. The sow will often also take to the tree, right behind the cubs. A brown bear, on the other hand, relies on strength and size to protect its offspring.

Do colors bother bears?

Not that I know of, but my advice is to dress in bright colors. While camping with my wife, we were berry picking, and I looked across the berry patch and saw a round black object down in the high brush, moving slowly. I looked through the scope of my field rifle and discovered that this object was my wife; she was dressed in a black sweater and was picking cranberries on her hands and knees. It's a good thing that I'm not a trigger-happy sportsman.

If you are in bear country, realize that ripe berry patches will attract bears. Stay out of the patches unless you can clearly see where you are at all times. Do not go on a blueberry-picking excursion if you cannot see what is ahead of you.

What about food in camp?

Never, ever keep food in your sleeping bag. Do not keep food where you are going to sleep. If your sleeping bag was in the car where there was food, get it well laundered before you take it into bear country. In the car, the bag picks up the scent of what anyone is eating—peanuts, popcorn, bacon, anything. This attracts bears, which have a very keen sense of smell. You invite trouble if you eat and sleep in the same place. Keep groceries a hundred yards from camp, preferably in a tree.

I can show cases in which people were bitten by disobeying this one simple rule. Two summers ago, some Boy Scouts were attacked while camping in Fairbanks. A youngster put a candy bar down in his sleeping bag when he went to bed. He awoke to find a bear chewing on his foot. He screamed in the dark and ran around the tent, trying to find the door. This awakened the other boys, and they also screamed and ran. As the kids tore by the bear, it nipped each one. The animal was scared. The kids were scared. The bear had followed the smell of chocolate to a large blue bag, which started to move when the bear went after it.

My advice is take food with little odor. If you must cook bacon, be sure that it is canned; then fry and eat it all, burn your can, crush it, and pack it out.

What about garbage?

Don't do what one foolish camper did: he left the garbage behind after pouring motor oil all over it. Bears, though, have been known to drink motor oil. I know three men who went into a restaurant adjacent to where they had been changing the oil in a car. They went in for lunch, stayed a long time, and left cans of opened motor oil unattended on the ground. I arrived on the scene to see a black bear lift a can of motor oil to his lips as though it were a can of soda pop.

Does playing dead work?

The majority of people who play dead are still around to talk about it. They say that as soon as they stopped fighting, the bear walked off and left them, or if it had picked them up, it dropped them. Most of the people who recover from a mauling insist that they were surprised by how strong the bear was and how soon they were too tired to fight any longer. They had to give up. Then the bear went off and left them. Let's say that you are being stalked, however. One bear by itself, circling your body and working its way toward where you are standing, is eventually going to pull you down. If you feel that you are being stalked for prey, you probably are. Normally, a bear will not eat a person; bears do not prefer human flesh. Many skeletons that we have found could have been persons stalked out of hunger, but this is difficult to prove. Sometimes, the bear discovers an already dead person and then starts to eat.

Are old bears easier to elude?

The opposite may be true. A hungry bear with poor teeth and failing eyesight that sees a human may want to eat him because it is easier than chasing salmon or going after a moose. Screaming and playing dead may do you some good, but that's doubtful. If you are being circled for food, you do not have much chance without a weapon.

Which kind of gun do you recommend carrying?

One that you can shoot. A cannon is no good if you cannot fire it. A lot depends on the person. Use at least a .30-06 caliber or larger gun with a heavy bullet. We do not recommend a bolt-action rifle because it is very slow to operate. Nor do we recommend a weapon with a scope on it. Open sights are much easier to use. A high-quality pump shotgun is easier for a non-hunter to handle than a rifle. Use slugs and not shot because shot is only good at close range.

We recommend shooting at five to seven yards. I would not recommend most handguns. When stalked, you need something powerful. I use a .45, one of the largest caliber handguns on the market. The better you can shoot, the better chance you will have.

What about bears that die hard?

Just because you shoot a bear, that is no guarantee it will die. One bear demolished two trucks in Alaska in 1974. It was sixteen years old, weighed nine hundred pounds, and crossed the highway at the wrong time. It had lived around Anchorage for most of its life and had spent its time between Fort Richardson Army Base and the Eagle River valley. We found .22 bullets in the bear. We found a dozen or more other projectiles, bits and pieces of buckshot, and birdshot. All had festered and healed over, and the bear went right on living.

What is the most unusual survival story you have heard?

This happened in the Arctic. An unarmed Eskimo woman fighting a bear stuck her mittened hand down the bear's throat. The mitten came off, and the bear choked and died. I do not know whether this is true, but it has been told up and down the Alaskan bush for years. There are other stories of bears being killed by people who used an ax.

Are small bears as dangerous as large bears?

Remember, you can't trust your estimate of a bear's size. There are times when all bears appear big. A man reported a grizzly to Alaskan troopers as being fifteen feet tall. It measured ten feet, dead. We get complaints that taxidermists have switched hides, giving the poor customer a smaller hide while keeping the larger one. Very few people can estimate a bear's height. Very ordinary bears can be ten-footers. Always act as though the bear you face is the swiftest and the most powerful bear anyplace.

How powerful are bears?

My home is on a mountainside outside of Anchorage, and we have bears all around us. Once, I followed a black bear that walked into my yard, looking for food. I had a piece of flatiron three-quarter-inch sheet steel, weighing more than five hundred pounds in the back of my truck. Flattened beneath it were bits of once-frozen herring and bait. The bear flipped the steel over his shoulder like a pencil to get at the fish. One year, I had a sack of fertilizer in the truck when a black bear came around, found the door ajar, yanked it open, went in after the container, and pulled it to the ground. Don't forget that bears are just as tough as they are strong. People in rural Alaska have a problem with bears breaking into their cabins. A man pounded two-inch nails, four inches apart, into the ramp leading to his home, to stick right into the bears' paws and tear their flesh if they tried to walk up into his house. One bear accepted the challenge, tromped right up the ramp with the nails protruding right into his paws, and then tried to break into the house. We advise people to be very cautious when they walk up to strange cabins in the woods. They literally have to watch their step.

Will all bears bite?

The idea is that you want to help the bear identify who you are. Normally, the bear will get interested in a moving object. Wave your arms; making noise is good. But if you are at twenty yards, those sudden actions can be threatening as far as the bear is concerned. You do not want to provoke an attack, and if you are so close that this happens, you had better have a weapon.

What about climbing a tree?

Not always such a good idea in Alaska. You cannot count on finding a huge, many-limbed spruce, which is ideal for climbing. Our trees are spindly, and in the North they fall over because of permafrost, meaning the roots cannot anchor on anything. A brown bear climbs a tree limb by limb, like a human. It does not dig in its claws and run up the tree like a black bear. You should know this difference.

How about climbing trees elsewhere?

If you must, then do it. Generally, you will not have time. One writer I know told his high-school students to pretend that he was a bear and to go climb something. He found that there would rarely be sufficient time to run, pick out a tree, and get far enough up it to escape a bear. On the other hand, six months ago an Alaskan fleeing a bear found his gun out of ammo and had to take to a tree. The bear was below him. The man had time to get into his pockets, reload the gun, and aim for a kill.

What about false charges?

I can show you cases in which a person attacked by a bear has stepped away and hid in the bushes, and the bear has charged right by. The chances are that this was not a false charge, but the man got off the trail and out of sight, and the bear, no longer seeing him, went right on to something else. You can never be certain about a false charge. Once, while my brother-in-law was visiting, he took our cocker spaniel into the woods for a walk. The dog was not restrained and went off barking at cubs in a tree until the sow went after the dog. The spaniel, as so often happens, took off after my brother-in-law for help; then, the bear started out after him. This is common, but the rest of what happened is not. My brother-in-law saw that the bear was closing rapidly and that he had no chance. So he ran a hundred yards and, with only seconds to spare, jumped off the trail and into high brush, where he hid. The bear went right on past him and never came back.

Is that typical?

In all of my research, I have never found a bear that has sniffed out an individual and gone after him, seeking him out. I cannot say that it does not happen, but I have not found it.

Can you kill a bear to protect your dog?

Alaskan law prohibits wanton killing of bears but does give you rights to protect life, limb, and property. If you kill, though, you are required to take hide and skull, make a written report to the Department of Fish and Game, give immediate notice to wildlife-enforcement officials, and surrender the hide. You may not keep it. The hides are sold to institutions or given to schools. Some are sold at auction.

Will bears always attack if surprised?

No. We had flown in to a small lake and had set up camp. I was moose hunting on a trail and keeping very quiet when all of a sudden a black bear fell out of the tree in front of me, landed on the ground, bounced like a ball, and then, terrified, headed for the hills. He was a young bear and probably had never seen a human before.

What about wearing a backpack?

Wear one. I have interviewed many people who, during a bear attack, went down, covered their vitals, and turned their faces to the ground while the bear took out its aggression on the backpack. As the bear was spending its energies chewing through the pack and destroying the equipment, the person had minutes trying to plan how to survive the ordeal. I can show case after case where this has happened. Recently, two surveyors working for the Bureau of Land Management were attacked in the field. These young people were severely mauled, but the gentleman had two packs on his back, one with heavy padding around thousands of dollars of surveying equipment. He did everything he could think of to keep the bear from flipping him over. His scalp was terribly torn, and the surgeon said that he had to be given two hundred stitches. But he lived to tell the story. If the packs had been off his back, he would have been another statistic.

What advice do you give to a person who meets a bear on a trail?

The question implies that there is a sudden meeting, so there isn't much time to run. Drop an item of clothing, a jacket or sweater. Many times, the bear will stop to investigate it, sniff it, and "work" it, and this buys time. "Out of sight, out of mind" isn't foolproof, but it does work. Delay the bear until you can get out of its view hoping it will go on about its business.

Do you have bears in Alaskan cities?

Yes, we do. In Anchorage, which has a population of about 260,000, bears are seen on the outskirts of town because they have been chased out of the high hills by construction and by bigger animals. The problem then becomes younger, inexperienced bears. Last summer, a docile bear was eating out of garbage cans in a fringe area. Neighbors had encouraged it. But one day, they reconsidered and got scared. They called enforcement officers to come and get their "problem." The officers went out at noon. People from nearby offices watched while several men killed the bear and hauled it away.

Are you partial to bears?

I try to be fair; it's a complex problem. The city has grown so rapidly in the past few years that we have taken over the bears' territory. I did it. My home is on top of a mountain outside the city. I bought my property in 1969, and when we started to build, we found a black bear den on the spot where I was to put my living room. It is common for us to see black and brown bears roaming through our yard, eighteen hundred feet up the mountainside. Sometimes they walk, and sometimes they sneak. One year, when the house was still being built, I watched two grizzlies sneak through the high grass on their stomachs, around the side of the house and up to the porch. A man standing in the grass who was unaccustomed to the habits of bears would never have seen their shrunken forms.

I respect bears. It is hard not to like them. I once accompanied a friend on a hunt to an island next to Kodiak. This man took a shot at a bear feeding on grass, missed, and it hit the earth next to it. The bear began digging where the bullet had stopped. The hunter took another shot and missed, and the bear jumped over to where that bullet had hit to start clawing the earth. This went on for fifteen minutes. The bear was in the business of chasing ground squirrels and apparently thought that the spinning dust and a shot had something to do with a squirrel. We got so amused that my friend decided he couldn't kill it. For more than an hour, we watched the bear enjoy itself in the sunshine. This incident helped me get involved in teaching to save the lives of bears as well as the lives of humans. Not every bear should be saved, but many of them don't need to be killed.

Do you agree with killing a bear in self-defense?

Sometimes, of course, it is necessary. I have done it in self-defense. While my wife and I were camping, I was sawing a tree not too far from our tent. She was down by the water. All of a sudden, I saw our tent shake as though some squirrels were jumping on it. I dropped the saw, went over, and didn't see anything, so I tried to get through the tent door. I am more than six feet tall and too big to easily wriggle through a tent flap, so I got down on all fours and poked my head inside. I couldn't see any squirrels but the tent was still bouncing up and down, so I backed out the door the way I had come in. At that precise moment the bear, which was alternately jumping on the outside of my tent and hiding in the woods, walked around the tent in back of me. There were two of us four yards apart on all fours, and one of us had to move faster than the other. Believe me, I shot. And fast. Self-defense can have many meanings. There are hundreds of bears killed each year in self-defense, but the majority of these killings, in my estimation, are not warranted.

What do you teach hunters?

We talk about how to pursue the bear, how to get the bear, and what to do after they have taken it. Most of the time, I teach individuals who are about to enter a strange land some basic rules of survival. It is very important to dispose of garbage properly. Burn it or pack it out. Don't keep leftovers; use canned goods, burn the cans, and pack the cans out. During the pipeline days, a husband and wife were camped along a river outside Valdez. Returning to the campsite at night, they were attacked and mauled. After being released from the hospital, they brought a lawsuit. They said that the state was at fault for not removing garbage from the campsite area, and the case went on for several days. We had nationally known bear experts testify on the habits of grizzlies to determine the conditions that led to the mauling. I was amazed to find that each person's testimony differed according to his own experience with a particular type of bear.

Are children taught bear survival?

For the most part, not at all. I have examined hundreds of books on bears and no two completely agree. Beyond that, in one school library, a book said the black bear was so docile that you need not consider it dangerous. Another book said that a white patch on a black bear was rare. In Alaska, almost all black bears have white under the chin. Black bears also are not always black; some are brown, some blue, and Canada has a black bear species that is predominantly white.

Are women more subject to attack during menstruation?

No, except in polar bear country. There, yes. According to recent experiments using different types of blood samples, it was discovered that menstrual blood made a difference to polar bears.

Is it an old wives' tale not to wear perfume?

Never wear perfume. Do not cover up human odor in bear country. The smell of a human will often make a bear flee in terror. To have that odor covered up could be your downfall. The perfume could attract a bear. Their noses are unbelievably powerful and accurate. One day, I took six good-size rainbow trout I had caught in the Deshka River, cleaned them, placed them into garbage bags for the night, lowered the bags into three feet of water, and anchored them with big rocks. Then, I went to my tent to sleep. When I got up in the morning and went for my fish, the bags were ripped and shredded. Not a fish scale remained. That brings up another point: don't throw dishwater with food in it willy-nilly. Wash dishes in streams, if available, or dump water in one spot—say, in the burial pit. Wash all utensils at once. Wash hands frequently.

Should people stay away from odd odors?

If you smell something decaying, you can bet that a bear smells it, too. Also, watch birds. If the ravens, eagles, and other sizeable scavengers repeatedly fly in one direction, something is dead and the bears are there.

Do you advocate the use of noisemakers?

I advocate noisemaking. Be aware of things you buy that make sounds with horns or whistles that could sound like a predator call or a distress or weakness call. There are small air horns on the market that squeak like an animal in distress. Avoid these.

Why do you advise people to examine bear droppings?

It is important to know what the bear is eating. As I have said, they eat anything. One home had cans of bug spray in the garage, and the bears got into the garage and ate through the cans. Several years ago, an Alaskan chopper crew hazed a bear to get him away from some surveyors. They didn't figure what was in store. The pilots landed the chopper later in the day and walked away from it. The hazed bear got to the helicopter, opened a door, got inside, chewed the seats, and devastated the aircraft. Bear droppings tell a great deal about what they've been up to. If you find bits of buttons, shoestrings, and coat collars, you had better take a warning.

The man in the photograph who was devoured except for his head, rib, and pelvic bones was a thirty-eight-year-old wildlife photographer who thought that he knew what he was doing. In August 1974 in Cold Bay, Alaska, he spent a week photographing brown bears to add to his collection. It was cold in his tent. He doffed his boots and clothes and slid into his sleeping bag, got warm, and slept. The tent fly may have moved from blasts of wind, and the tent occasionally shuddered enough that a bear feeding on salmon in a nearby stream was either annoyed or attracted by the tent, approached it, and smelled the man and some food. The photographer awakened, felt the tent move, and decided that he might have set the tent too close to the bears' feeding grounds. The bear roared, and the tent gave way under six hundred pounds of brown bear. The man slipped out, sprinted down the road, and looked back to see the bear ripping the tent and its contents. Then, the animal saw the man. The bear's paws were eight and half inches across. It charged, swatted the man to the ground, and in minutes had completed its mission. It dragged the man to the nearest alder clump and started to feed. The next day, all that was found was a belt, shirt, pants, a couple of ribs, part of the pelvis, and part of the head. The bear was killed, and its stomach was examined. It contained plastic bags and human skin, bones, and hair. An official report noted that the man had made two significant errors: He'd had food in his tent, and he had camped on a bear trail on the bank of a major salmon stream. Learn from his mistakes.